G000253611

50 Walks in
EDINBURGH & EASTERN SCOTLAND

First published 2003
Researched and written by Rebecca Ford

Produced by AA Publishing
© Automobile Association Developments Limited 2003
Illustrations © Automobile Association Developments Limited 2003
Reprinted 2007

Published by AA Publishing (a trading name of Automobile
Association Developments Limited, whose registered office is Fanum
House, Basing View, Basingstoke, Hampshire RG21 4EA;
registered number 1878835)

This product includes mapping data licensed
from Ordnance Survey® with the permission of
the Controller of Her Majesty's Stationery Office.
© Crown copyright 2007. All rights reserved. Licence number
100021153

ISBN-10: 0-7495-3624-1
ISBN 13: 978-0-7495-3624-4

A03349

A CIP catalogue record for this book is available
from the British Library.

Visit the AA Publishing website at www.theAA.com/travel

Paste-up and editorial by Outcrop Publishing Services Ltd, Cumbria
for AA Publishing

Colour reproduction by LC Repro
Printed in Italy by G. Canale & C. SpA, Torino, Italy

Legend

←-------	Walk route	P	Car park
•••••••	Optional walk route		Cliff
-------	Adjoining footpath		Rock outcrop
—·—·—	County boundary		Beach
☼	Viewpoint	♣ ♧	Woodland
▲392	Spot height		Parkland
▨	Built-up area	†	Church, cathedral, chapel
●	Place of interest	WC	Toilet
△	Steep section	🛆	Picnic area

Edinburgh & Eastern Scotland locator map

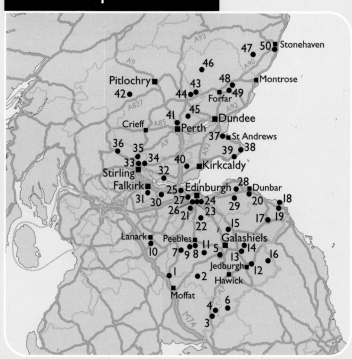

Contents

Contents

Contents

Rating: Each walk is rated for its relative difficulty compared to the other walks in this book. Walks marked 🚶 🚶 🚶 are likely to be shorter and easier with little total ascent. The hardest walks are marked 🚶 🚶 🚶 .

Walking in Safety: For advice and safety tips ➤ 128.

Introducing Edinburgh & Eastern Scotland

The glen was deserted. The only sounds I could hear were the chattering of the river and the whisper of the summer wind. I took the path that ran uphill from the sleepy little church, and followed it as it snaked its way on to the moors. The heather was in bloom, quilting the lonely uplands in a bouncy blanket of purple, amethyst and mauve. I walked briskly, breathing in the crystal air – unaccompanied save for the occasional skylark or delicately painted butterfly. In the distance rose a range of hills, their sides etched with craggy rocks that had been weathered by thousands of years of ice, and snow, and rain. Eventually I reached a sheepfold, a neat circle of deep grey stones that had been hewn into blocks by unknown hands and somehow carried on to this isolated moor. This would be a harsh place in winter – but in summer it was a delight…

There are lots of places like this in eastern Scotland – places where you can escape the crowds and walk through countryside that still seems to belong to nature rather than man.

Too few people explore this part of Scotland, at least on foot, as they seem to feel that walking in Scotland means the Highlands. Of course, it's true that the Highlands offer the wildest walking – but the variety, the history and the coastline of the east are more than adequate compensation.

This is a vast area and encompasses a deliciously varied range of landscapes: you'll find everything from historic cobbled streets in Edinburgh to narrow sheep tracks on the Eildon Hills. There is walking here to suit all tastes and abilities, whether you like a gentle ramble through the fields or a strenuous hike up a hill. There are plenty of footpaths and a number of waymarked, long distance trails cut through the countryside. You can follow sections of the Southern Upland Way, which runs 212 miles (341km) from Portpatrick in the west to Cockburnspath in the east; the Pennine Way (270 miles/435km) which has its northern terminus at Kirk Yetholm in the Borders; and St Cuthbert's Way (62 miles/100km), from Melrose to Lindisfarne. You can also follow old drove roads, along which herds of cattle were driven to market; or walk along Dere Street, an old Roman road.

The scenery here shows surprising variations in character. The rolling hills of the south west feel remote and lonely, while the borderlands to the east have a pastoral appeal, dominated by the mighty Tweed and dotted with mature trees and historic abbeys like Dryburgh and Melrose. The coastline

---

PUBLIC TRANSPORT   ⓘ

Many walks in this book are only accessible by car. However, there are regular train services from Edinburgh to Stirling, Dunblane, Linlithgow, Falkirk and Perth. For national rail enquiries, phone 0845 748 4950 or visit www.nationalrail.co.uk; for Scottish Citylink (bus and coach) phone 08705 505050 or visit www.citylink.demon.co.uk; for Traveline phone 0870 608 2 608 or visit www.traveline.org.uk.

has a different appeal, with dark sandy beaches and dramatic cliffs that support vast colonies of seabirds.

The city of Edinburgh has lots to offer the walker, for not only are its streets picturesque and full of history (this was where Burke and Hare, the body-snatchers, once operated), it is also surrounded by the Pentland Hills. From Edinburgh, you cross the Forth Bridge to the ancient kingdom of Fife, where you can follow the Coastal Path, which runs through pretty fishing villages like Anstruther and Crail. West of Fife is the heart of Scotland – Perthshire, where the landscape becomes wilder. This is the Scotland of everyone's dreams, with moody castles and brooding hills.

The north east is different again. In Angus you can explore peaceful glens, such as Glen Prosen, or visit Kirriemuir, where J M Barrie, Peter Pan's creator, was born. Further north is the Howe of the Mearns, immortalised in the books of Lewis Grassic Gibbon; and then – well, get those boots on and find out...

Using this Book

Information panels

An information panel for each walk shows its relative difficulty (➤ 5), the distance and total amount of ascent. An indication of the gradients you will encounter is shown by the rating ▲▲▲ (no steep slopes) to ▲▲▲ (several very steep slopes).

Maps

There are 30 maps, covering 40 of the walks. Some walks have a suggested option in the same area. The information panel for these walks will tell you how much extra walking is involved. On short-cut suggestions the panel will tell you the total distance if you set out from the start of the main walk. Where an option returns to the same point on the main walk, just the distance of the loop is given. Where an option leaves the main walk at one point and returns to it at another, then the distance shown is for the whole walk. The minimum time suggested is for reasonably fit walkers and doesn't allow for stops. Each walk has a suggested map. Laminated aqua3 maps are longer lasting and water resistant.

Start Points

The start of each walk is given as a six-figure grid reference prefixed by two letters indicating which 100km square of the National Grid it refers to. You'll find more information on grid references on most Ordnance Survey maps.

Dogs

We have tried to give dog owners useful advice about how dog friendly each walk is. Please respect other countryside users. Keep your dog under control, especially around livestock, and obey local bylaws and other dog control notices.

Car Parking

Many of the car parks suggested are public, but occasionally you may find you have to park on the roadside or in a lay-by. Please be considerate when you leave your car, ensuring that access roads or gates are not blocked and that other vehicles can pass safely. Remember that pub car parks are private and should not be used unless you have the owner's permission.

Walk 1

A Beefy Devil of a Walk in Moffat

A hearty walk around the intriguingly named Devil's Beef Tub near the small town of Moffat.

·DISTANCE·	4½ miles (7.2km)
·MINIMUM TIME·	2hrs
·ASCENT / GRADIENT·	1,076ft (328m) ▲▲▲
·LEVEL OF DIFFICULTY·	👫 👫 👫
·PATHS·	Grassy moorlands and firm farm tracks
·LANDSCAPE·	Dramatic gully and extensive views of borderlands
·SUGGESTED MAP·	aqua3 OS Explorer 330 Moffat & St Mary's Loch
·START / FINISH·	Grid reference: NT 055127
·DOG FRIENDLINESS·	Keep on lead as plenty of sheep
·PARKING·	By forest access gate
·PUBLIC TOILETS·	None on route; nearest off High Street in Moffat

BACKGROUND TO THE WALK

Dark, forbidding and dramatic (Sir Walter Scott once described it as a 'black, blackguard-looking abyss of a hole'), the hollow known as the Devil's Beef Tub has a history as turbulent as its name suggests. Over the years this deep, natural bowl has been used as a hiding place by thieves, formed a refuge for the persecuted and witnessed feats of daring – and even murder.

Once known as the Corrie of Annan, it gained the name the Devil's Beef Tub in the 16th century when it was frequently used by the Johnstone clan, a local reiving (rustling) family, to hide stolen cattle after a raid. In reference to this it was also sometimes sardonically referred to as the Marquis of Annandale's Beef Stand.

The Covenanting Movement
The tub was not only useful for sheltering stolen animals, however – it was also used as a hideout by persecuted Covenanters during Charles II's so-called 'Killing Times'. The origins of the covenanting movement went back to the time when bishops were imposed on the Church of Scotland by James VI. Years later his son, Charles I, who also believed in the Divine Right of Kings, tried to interfere further in Scottish ecclesiastical affairs. This provoked such hostility that there was a riot in Edinburgh, resulting in the signing of the National Covenant in 1638. This document affirmed the authority of the Church of Scotland over the King in all spiritual matters and was circulated throughout Scotland, gaining particular support in the south west.

Throughout the 17th century, religious fanaticism grew and Covenanters became a powerful force in Scotland. When Charles II, who had Roman Catholic sympathies, was restored to the throne he tried to suppress the movement. There were many battles and prisoners were often brutally treated. Finding themselves outlawed, some ministers of the Church began holding illegal services, known as 'conventicles', in the open air. Persecution only fuelled resistance and during the years 1684–7, the 'Killing Times', hundreds of people were slaughtered by officers of the Crown. The most notorious of these was Graham of Claverhouse, later Viscount Dundee. There's a reminder of these violent times near the car park at the Devil's Beef Tub, where you can see a stone dedicated to John Hunter, a Covenanter who was shot on the hills here in 1685.

A Rebel in The Tub

This violent period in history came to an end when James II's son-in-law, William of Orange, came to the throne in 1689 – but was soon replaced in the following century by the violence of the Jacobite Rebellion. In 1746 a prisoner from the Battle of Culloden, which had brought the rebellion to an end the previous year, was being marched to Carlisle for trial. He escaped his guards by leaping into the Devil's Beef Tub and disappearing in the swirling mist. Once again this great hollow had played its part in Scottish history.

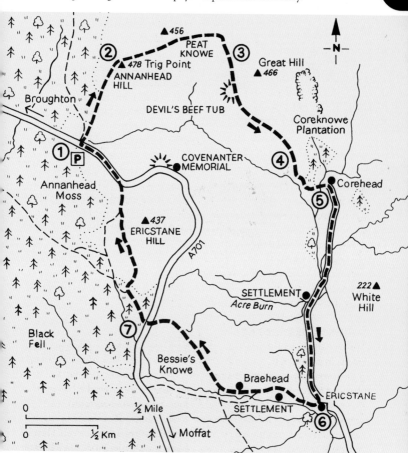

Walk 1 **Directions**

① From the forest gateway on the **A701**, go through the wooden gate on the right-hand side, then climb the wooden fence ahead. You now start to ascend the grassy slope of **Annanhead Hill**, keeping to the right of the two wire fences as you walk up to reach the trig point on the summit.

Walk 1

② Bear right over **Peat Knowe**, keeping the wall and fence to your left. You then follow the path down the grassy slope to the head of a gully, where your path meets the wall. Walk to the other side of the gully, then turn right and pick your way to the edge to enjoy the views over the **Devil's Beef Tub**.

WHERE TO EAT AND DRINK ⓘ

Moffat's just a short drive away and has plenty of places to choose from. Among them is the **Balmoral Hotel** on the main square, which serves bar meals such as fish and chips, and the **Ariffe Café**, also on the square, which serves teas, ices and snacks. If you've got a sweet tooth you can also investigate the **Moffat Toffee Shop**, which sells a wide range of traditional sticky sweets.

---

③ Now follow the narrow path as it continues to descend, walking over grass and bracken – you'll get good views down into the valley. Eventually you'll reach an area of pasture, in front of a plantation. Walk to the two gates and go through the metal gate on the right.

④ Continue downhill on the grassy bank, then go through the gate and along the rough track, swinging left round the wall of the plantation. Go through the gate behind the red-brick house, then continue towards the farm buildings. Walk between the buildings on to the

---

WHAT TO LOOK FOR ⓘ

Long before the days of the Border Reivers and the Covenanters, this area of Scotland was part of the Roman Empire. **Ericstane Hill**, which you pass on the latter part of this walk, was the site of a Roman signal station. It was used to monitor and coordinate troop movements along the Roman road that stretched from Carlisle to the Clyde.

---

tarmac track and towards the timber barn, continuing ahead to join a farm road.

⑤ You now follow that farm road along the valley bottom. Keep an eye out for a small area of undulating land on your right – it's all that remains of an ancient settlement. Eventually you'll reach **Ericstane farm**.

⑥ Turn right, now, through a gate, then head uphill on a stony track, with woodland on your left. You'll soon pass an area of pronounced banks and ditches – another reminder of a former settlement – and will then come to a house. Shortly after the farmhouse, go through a gate, then turn sharp right, following the track as it runs by a stone wall. Eventually you'll reach the main road, where you cross over – take care as it's busy – and go through a gate.

WHILE YOU'RE THERE ⓘ

Moffat has several historical associations. Robert Burns wrote one of his poems at the Black Bull Hotel and Graham of Claverhouse, the scourge of the Covenanters, once stayed here. Of more recent interest is the fact that the town was the birthplace of Air Chief Marshal Lord Dowding, who led Fighter Command in the Battle of Britain.

---

⑦ Your route now takes you over **Ericstane Hill**. Bear right and follow the track as it runs north round the far side of the hill. The track is rather indistinct in places, covered in grass and reeds. Keep to the left of the summit, walking around the brow of the hill to rejoin the road. Turn right here if you'd like to visit the **Covenanter memorial**, or turn left to return to the start of the walk.

Going the Whole Hogg in Ettrick

An enjoyable tramp in the footsteps of a local poet.

•DISTANCE•	4½ miles (7.2km)
•MINIMUM TIME•	2hrs 30min
•ASCENT / GRADIENT•	689ft (210m) ▲▲▲
•LEVEL OF DIFFICULTY•	林 林 林
•PATHS•	Narrow hill tracks, moorland and waymarked trail, 4 stiles
•LANDSCAPE•	Open rolling hills and sleepy valley
•SUGGESTED MAP•	aqua3 OS Explorer 330 Moffat & St Mary's Loch
•START / FINISH•	Grid reference: NT 265144
•DOG FRIENDLINESS•	Plenty of interesting smells but keep on lead near sheep
•PARKING•	By village hall on minor road west of B709
•PUBLIC TOILETS•	None on route

BACKGROUND TO THE WALK

> *'For mony a day, frae sun to sun,*
> *We've toil'd an helpit ane anither;*
> *An' mony a thousand mile thou'st run,*
> *To keep my thraward flocks thegither'*
>
> from *The Mountain Bard*, 1807

Those lines are taken from *The Author's Address to his Auld Dog Hector*, one of the many poems written by James Hogg, a shepherd turned writer who was born in this tranquil valley in 1770. Even if you aren't sure of the meaning of some of the words, you can't help but be touched by the obvious love the poet has for his dog. It's easy to imagine the two of them pacing the same tracks that you follow on this walk.

Monument to a Shepherd

Hogg is popularly known as the Ettrick Shepherd and you'll pass a monument to him on this walk. However, he would probably prefer to be remembered by his work, as his literary achievements are considerable – particularly for someone who had such humble origins. The son of a poor farmer, he hardly received any formal education – indeed, some reports state that his schooling lasted no more than six months. By the age of seven he had started work as a cowherd on a farm.

But he had both ambition and determination. He also had an artistic streak, perhaps inherited from his grandfather, said to have been the last man who could speak to the fairies. By the time Hogg reached his mid-teens he was working as a shepherd and had taught himself to read and write. He began composing poetry while out on the hills with his flock, drawing on the tradition of local ballads that he had learned from his mother. He soon came to the attention of Sir Walter Scott, who was travelling the Borders, and the two became friends. Scott became Hogg's mentor – although the pronounced differences in their class meant that Scott always regarded him as a bit of a peasant.

Walk 2

Success Breeds Success

Hogg modelled himself on Robert Burns and began to get his poems and songs published. His first collection of ballads, *The Mountain Bard* (1807), was well received and three years later Hogg moved to Edinburgh to try and make it as a writer. Within a few years he had been recognised as one of the leading poets of the day – the poor country shepherd had become a celebrity.

After a few years Hogg returned to the Borders, where he wrote the work for which he is best remembered – *The Private Memoirs and Confessions of a Justified Sinner* (1824). Contemporary critics felt it was so sophisticated that it could never have been written by such an uneducated man.

James Hogg was eventually offered a knighthood, but his wife made him turn it down. He died in 1835 and is buried in Ettrick churchyard.

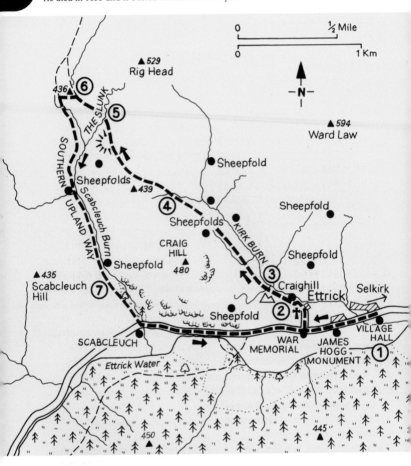

Walk 2 **Directions**

① From the parking place by the **village hall**, turn left along the road past the monument to James Hogg and up to the **war memorial**. Turn right and walk past the church, then take the track that bears sharp left past the farm buildings. Go through the metal gate, then fork left at the right of way sign.

② Walk uphill now, following the track through another gate and up the grassy slope – it's quite a puff, but think of how firm your thighs will be! There's a **monument** on the hill above, which you keep to your left. Follow the narrow track, passing a circular sheepfold on your left and two on the opposite hillside on the right.

③ Your path now skirts around **Craig Hill**, roughly following the **Kirk Burn**. Keep an eye out for another circular sheepfold on your left, then two more away to the right. At this point the track disappears and the ground becomes more boggy underfoot. Don't be tempted by the track that bears left but maintain your direction, heading for the low ground ahead.

WHILE YOU'RE THERE ⓘ

Tibbie Shiels Inn, on the A708, is an extremely well-known watering hole which attracts visitors because of its literary connections. Tibbie was the wife of a local mole-catcher and ran this isolated inn for many years. She must have pulled a good pint because it was a favourite haunt of Sir Walter Scott, who would often drink here with his friend James Hogg.

---

④ Keep walking over the moorland – passing a lone fence post on your left, then a circular, stone sheepfold, also on your left-hand side but further away. In summer you might see wild flowers such as early purple orchids and marsh orchids. Continue towards **The Slunk**, a heavily eroded burn, from where you get great views back up the Ettrick Valley.

⑤ You'll now have to scramble down the banks of The Slunk, and cross over the water – there are some rocks to help you across, but be careful. Your way then takes you over to meet a wire fence. Here, you bear left and follow the line of the fence to reach the metal fingerpost marked 'Riskinhope'.

WHAT TO LOOK FOR ⓘ

You pass **Ettrick kirk** – or church – early on in this walk. It dates from 1824, probably replacing earlier ones as the parish has been here for at least 800 years. Do go inside if the church is open, otherwise take a peek in the graveyard, as this is the burial place of James Hogg.

---

⑥ At the fingerpost, cross the stile and continue descending along the other side of the fence to meet the **Southern Upland Way**. Cross back over the fence at the wooden stile, then bear left on the wide path as it runs back down to the **Ettrick Valley**. You'll pass two particularly well-maintained sheepfolds along the way, and will then come to a stone stile.

⑦ Nip over this stile to enter a pasture, then go down to meet the road at the bottom left-hand corner. Cross another stone stile here and drop into the lane opposite **Scabcleuch farm**. Turn left again over the bridge and walk back to the war memorial. Walk past the monument and return to the parking place at start of the walk.

WHERE TO EAT AND DRINK ⓘ

The best place to try is the **Tushielaw Inn** which is a few miles further north on the B709. It's got a pleasant atmosphere and offers simple bar lunches such as ploughman's lunches and sausage and chips, and also serves more substantial meals in the evening. Alternatively you can try **Tibbie Shiels Inn** on the A708, which does lunches, high tea and dinner.

Walk 3

A Poet's Passions at Langholm

An exhilarating climb is followed by a more gentle stroll past Hugh MacDiarmid's memorial.

•DISTANCE•	3 miles (4.8km)
•MINIMUM TIME•	1hr 30min
•ASCENT / GRADIENT•	919ft (280m) ▲▲▲
•LEVEL OF DIFFICULTY•	然 然 然
•PATHS•	Firm hill tracks and tarmac roads
•LANDSCAPE•	Lush green borderlands and fine views
•SUGGESTED MAP•	aqua3 OS Explorer 323 Eskdale & Castle O'er Forest
•START / FINISH•	Grid reference: NY 364845
•DOG FRIENDLINESS•	Keep on lead as there are plenty of sheep
•PARKING•	On main street in Langholm
•PUBLIC TOILETS•	Off main street of Langholm

BACKGROUND TO THE WALK

The Scots have long been passionate about their independence and take great pride in their rich culture. On this walk, in which you climb high above the little town of Langholm, you'll pass a memorial to one of the founding fathers of the modern Scottish nationalist movement – the poet Hugh MacDiarmid.

A Cultural Giant

MacDiarmid, whose real name was Christopher Murray Grieve, was born in Langholm in 1892 and is considered one of Scotland's leading 20th-century poets, ranking alongside Robert Burns in cultural importance. His early working life was spent in journalism, working in Montrose and London, and he then turned to writing poetry. A man of passionate views – he was a communist and nationalist – his verses were written in local dialect, mixed with words taken from the older Scottish tongue. His volumes of poetry included *Sangschaw*, his first book which was published in 1925; *Penny Wheep* (1926) and *A Drunk Man Looks at the Thistle* (1926). His works sparked a revival of interest in Scottish language and culture and he became a central figure in the country's literary revival.

Championing Home Rule

During the 1930s he moved to Shetland, where he continued to write. He made a great impression on those who met him there and was once described as: 'Unmistakably the genius, with tensely thoughtful features and smouldering, deep-set eyes… (he is) almost rustically Scots… wearing a kilt and a plaid, both of bright tartan.' Years later another writer was to describe him as 'a magnificent mouse of a man'. He was by this time involved in the early nationalist movement, which had started in Scotland after the First World War and grew in strength during the 1920s. Together with other writers, such as Lewis Spence and Neil Gunn, MacDiarmid voiced a desire for Home Rule for Scotland. The movement grew into the Scottish National Party which was formed in 1934.

After the Second World War, MacDiarmid moved back to the Borders, living with his wife in a two room labourer's cottage near Biggar. It was simple in the extreme and had no water or electricity, but it was from here that he embarked on lecture tours all over the world. He would often travel to Edinburgh, where he would drink with other Scottish writers like Norman MacCaig and Sorley MacLean.

MacDiarmid died in 1978, his love of Scotland as passionate as ever. He was buried in Langholm, against the wishes of the local 'gentry' who disliked his radical views. Above the door of his old home are inscribed the words:

> *'The rose of all the world is not for me*
> *I want for my part*
> *Only the little white rose of Scotland*
> *That smells sharp and sweet and breaks the heart'*

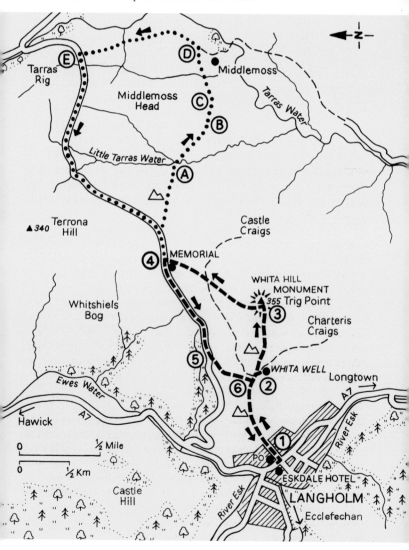

Walk 3

Walk 3 Directions

① From the **post office** on the main street, turn left and take the path next to it that runs uphill. Go through the gate at the top. Follow the grassy track that continues ahead to reach a green seat beside **Whita Well**, a natural spring.

WHERE TO EAT AND DRINK ⓘ

The **Eskdale Hotel**, at the very end of this walk, is a friendly place and serves a good selection of bar food, from light meals like baked potatoes to more substantial meals such as chops. They're also happy to do tea and biscuits. Next door is the **Flo'er O' Eskdale**, a coffee shop that serves toasties, scones and sandwiches (closed on Sundays).

---

② Now take the track just to the left of the seat, running steeply up the hill. Follow this track as it runs under the line of pylons and up to the top of **Whita Hill**. There are stone steps taking you up to the monument, a 100ft (30m) high **obelisk** commemorating Sir John Malcolm, a once-famous soldier, diplomat and scholar. From here you'll get great views – and on a clear day you can even see the peaks of the Lake District.

③ From the monument, walk down a few paces to join the wide footpath that runs in front of it, then turn right. It's easy walking now, following this clear track downhill with heather on the slopes to either side. Eventually you'll reach an unusual metal **sculpture** on the left-hand side. The sculpture, which is meant to resemble an open book, was created by Jake Harvey and is a memorial to Hugh MacDiarmid. There's a small cairn there too.

④ Go through the metal gate by the sculpture and turn left. You now simply follow the road as it winds downhill – it's quite a long stretch but it's fairly quiet. Go back under the line of electricity pylons then, just after you pass a copse on your right-hand side, take the track on the left – it's signposted 'Langholm Walks 10'.

⑤ You now follow this footpath, which is lined with wild grasses and thistles – it's a great place to spot butterflies in the summer. Eventually the footpath becomes less distinct and runs through a small boggy patch. After this you soon return to the gate you reached on your outward journey.

⑥ Turn right, through the gate, and walk down the hill, past the golf course and back into the town. It's quite a steep descent and could be slippery in bad weather. If you're here in the summer you should be able to spot red clover lining the path – this really attracts the bees. Eventually you'll reach the main street in Langholm, with a hotel and a coffee shop ahead.

WHILE YOU'RE THERE ⓘ

Not far from Langholm is the delightfully named town of **Ecclefechan**. This was the birthplace of Thomas Carlyle (1795–1881). An historian, critic and essayist, Carlyle was one of the most influential thinkers of the 19th century. His house is now a small museum and contains some personal memorabilia. About 8 miles (12.9km) north of Langholm, where the White Esk meets the Black Esk, was once the location for the local **Handfasting Fair**. This was held every August from the 16th to the 18th century. Unmarried couples would pair off for a year's trial marriage – and return to the fair the following year to declare whether they would get married or part.

And on Across the Moors

A loop that takes you to a remote farm.
See map and information panel for Walk 3

Walk 4

•DISTANCE•	3½ miles (5.7km)
•MINIMUM TIME•	1hr 30min
•ASCENT / GRADIENT•	427ft (130m) ▲▲▲
•LEVEL OF DIFFICULTY•	林 林 林

Walk 4 Directions (Walk 3 option)

From Point ④ on the main walk, turn right and walk over the cattle grid. After about 100yds (91m) bear to your right, away from the road, and follow the narrow track that plunges steeply down the hill, running parallel with the wall on the right-hand side. There's lots of bracken covering the slopes.

Eventually you'll come down through a burn (Point Ⓐ), where your path bears right. Cross the stream and follow the track with the stream running beside you on the left. Where another channel joins from the left (Point Ⓑ) continue in the same direction to reach a wall (Point Ⓒ). Turn left now and follow the wall until you come up to a house on the right-hand side. Climb over the metal gate, keep walking with the wall on your right, and walk close to the house where you then clamber over another gate. Keep walking, hop over the next gate and join the wide firm track (Point Ⓓ).

You now turn left, following the track past a line of telegraph poles on the left-hand side – there are sheep here, so watch your dog. You'll eventually go over a small bridge and will come on to the main road (Point Ⓔ).

Turn left and walk along the road. Traffic does come along here but it is generally fairly quiet. On the right-hand side are areas where peat is cut for use by local people as fuel. Your path will start to climb uphill and you'll eventually come back to the **MacDiarmid monument** where you rejoin the main walk at Point ④.

WHAT TO LOOK FOR   ⓘ

Take a look at the **Town Head Bridge** in Langholm. Thomas Telford (1757–1834) was involved in its construction when he was a journeyman. He was born in Dumfriesshire, the son of a local shepherd who died when Thomas was only three months old. Telford served an apprenticeship as a stonemason in Langholm and trained himself to be an architect. He moved on to Edinburgh in order to work on the building of the New Town, and later went to London. Telford, who is one of Scotland's greatest engineers, is most famous as a bridge builder, but he also carried out many road surveys. This gave him the nickname 'Colossus of Roads'. It was he who surveyed the Carlisle–Glasgow road – one of the motorways of its day. He is buried in Westminster Abbey.

Walk 5

From Selkirk to… Africa

A gentle walk by Ettrick Water, laced with memories of a great explorer.

•DISTANCE•	3 miles (4.8km)
•MINIMUM TIME•	1hr 40min
•ASCENT / GRADIENT•	131ft (40m) ▲▲▲
•LEVEL OF DIFFICULTY•	🏃 🏃 🏃
•PATHS•	Riverside paths and woodland tracks, town streets, 4 stiles
•LANDSCAPE•	Gentle, wooded riverbanks and historic town
•SUGGESTED MAP•	aqua3 OS Explorer 338 Galashiels, Selkirk & Melrose
•START / FINISH•	Grid reference: NT 469284
•DOG FRIENDLINESS•	Good – but don't let them chase ducks
•PARKING•	West Port Car Park in Selkirk
•PUBLIC TOILETS•	By car park

Walk 5 Directions

It is hard to imagine that the sleepy town of Selkirk has any connection to the wilds of Africa. But look carefully at the statue in the High Street and you'll see that it commemorates Mungo Park, a local man and noted explorer. Park, who was born in 1771 and educated at Selkirk Grammar School, trained as a doctor. But instead of settling down to a comfortable life, he took a post as surgeon's mate on a ship bound for the East Indies. It gave him a taste for travel. He returned from the voyage – and promptly set off again, this time heading for Africa to map the Niger.

WHILE YOU'RE THERE ⓘ

Bowhill, home of the Duke of Buccleuch and Queensberry, is 3 miles (4.8km) west of Selkirk on the A708. It's a Georgian house stuffed with art treasures as well as elegant furniture, silver and porcelain. It's a good place to bring children as they've also got a restored Victorian kitchen and a country park with an adventure area and nature trails.

From the statue of Park, walk to the **Market Place**, then turn left down **Ettrick Terrace**, go left at the church, then sharp right down **Forest Road**. Follow this downhill, cutting off the corners using the steps, to come on to **Mill Street**. Go right, then left on to **Buccleuch Road**. Turn right following the signs for the riverside walk and walk across **Victoria Park** to join a tarmac track.

Turn left, walk by the river, then join the road and continue to cross the bridge. Turn left along **Ettrickhaugh Road**, passing a row of cottages on your left. Just past the cottages turn left, cross a tiny footbridge, then take the indistinct track on the left. Walk to the riverbank, then turn right.

It's a gentle walk beside the river – very different to Park's extraordinary journey, which lasted over 2½ years. Not only did he become desperately ill, he was even captured and held prisoner by a tribal leader. He escaped after four months and continued his travels, following the Niger to Sillis and only abandoning his journey when he became too ill to carry on. When he returned to Scotland he published an account of his travels, got married and took a post as a doctor in Peebles. You'd think he would have had enough excitement to last the rest of his life, but Park longed to return to Africa. As Sir Walter Scott later wrote: 'He would rather brave Africa and all its horrors, than wear out his life in long and toilsome rides over the hills in Scotland…'

Now follow the path along the river margin – it's eroded in places. Eventually you join a wider track and bear left. You soon reach a weir and a salmon ladder. Turn right to cross the tiny bridge.

WHAT TO LOOK FOR ℹ

You've got a great chance of seeing a **dipper** on this walk, particularly at the point where Ettrick and Yarrow Waters meet. Also known as the water ouzel, the dipper's a pretty little brown bird with a white breast. It feeds on insects, often wading through rushing water and bobbing up and down while searching for them – hence its name.

Immediately after this go left and continue walking alongside the river until you reach a point at which the **Yarrow Water** joins the **Ettrick Water** – a good spot for a snooze if it's sunny. I don't know whether Park ever came here, but it's perfectly possible. He might even have come with George Scott and Alexander Anderson, friends of his from Selkirk who accompanied him when he set sail again for Africa in 1805, with the intention of completing the journey along the Niger. They never came home. Scott and Anderson died from fever. Park

continued without them, writing: 'I shall … discover the termination of the Niger or perish in the attempt.'

Now retrace your steps for a short distance, then turn left at a crossing of tracks. Walk through the woods, cross over the bridge by the weir again, then take the path to the left. Follow the track round the meadow to reach the mill buildings. Bear right (don't cross the bridge) and continue, walking with the **mill lade** (small canal) on your left. Where the path splits, take the track on the left to follow a straight, concrete path beside the water. At the **fish farm**, walk around the buildings, then bear left to continue following the mill lade. Go left over the footbridge, then right, passing the cottages again. At the main road go right to reach the bridge.

Don't cross the bridge but take the path on the left. This leads you past a sports ground, then skirts a housing estate. Follow it until you reach the pedestrian footbridge on your right, where you cross the river, bear right and then retrace your steps over **Victoria Park** and uphill to the **Market Place**. Mungo Park did continue his journey, but disappeared in the jungle. His family searched for him, but it was not until years later that they discovered he had drowned while trying to escape from hostile tribesmen. He never reached the source of the Niger.

WHERE TO EAT AND DRINK ℹ

There are a few places in Selkirk. Among the hotels serving bar meals is the **Cross Keys** by the Market Place, which serves toasted sandwiches and light meals. There's also a small tea room. Look out for the famous Selkirk bannock, too – it's a type of fruit bread.

Walk 6

Remembering the Reivers at Newcastleton

A quiet walk through borderlands where cattle raiding was once a part of everyday life for the local inhabitants.

•DISTANCE•	5 miles (8km)
•MINIMUM TIME•	2hrs
•ASCENT / GRADIENT•	689ft (210m) ▲▲ ▲▲ ▲
•LEVEL OF DIFFICULTY•	🚶 🚶🚶 🚶🚶
•PATHS•	Quiet byroads and farm tracks, one rough climb
•LANDSCAPE•	Rolling borderlands and moors
•SUGGESTED MAP•	aqua3 OS Explorer 324 Liddesdale & Kershope Forest
•START / FINISH•	Grid reference: NY 483875
•DOG FRIENDLINESS•	Can mostly run free, Carby Hill not good for older dogs
•PARKING•	Douglas Square
•PUBLIC TOILETS•	Langholm Street, next to fire station

BACKGROUND TO THE WALK

It might seem quiet today, but the area around Newcastleton was once what tabloid newspapers would now describe as 'war-torn'. Ownership of these borderlands was hotly disputed between England and Scotland for hundreds of years and there were frequent battles and skirmishes. You'll pass a reminder of those turbulent days on this walk.

Raids and Revenge
Because places like Newcastleton were so remote from the centres of power in both London and Edinburgh, they were not only difficult to defend, they also had a reputation for lawlessness. Feuds often developed between powerful local families and violent raids, and cases of cattle rustling (reiving), were common – cattle were then a valuable asset. These were ruthless people who could probably have shown the Vikings a thing or two about raping and pillaging.

A raid would commonly be followed by an illegal revenge attack (which of course was better fun, being illegal) or sometimes a legal 'Hot Trod'. This was a pursuit mounted immediately after a raid and had strict rules – including one stating that a lighted turf had to be carried if the trod crossed the border. When reivers were caught they were often taken hostage (the ransom money was very handy), taken prisoner, or even killed. Not surprisingly the countryside became studded with sturdy castles and fortified 'pele' towers, so that people could better defend themselves.

The most powerful family in this area were the Armstrongs, the principal reiving clan in the Borders. They were extremely influential and held large tracts of land. Their main seat was Mangerton Tower, the rather pitiful remains of which you can see on this walk. The Armstrongs were said to be able to muster 3,000 mounted men whenever they wished to launch a raid into England. They were ruthless and violent, running a rather successful protection racket as one of their money-making ventures. Imagine the mafia with cows and you'll get the picture.

Controlling the Clans

It wasn't until the Union of the Crowns took place in 1603, following the death of Queen Elizabeth I, that the Border wars ceased and the power of the reiving clans was finally dispersed. Keen to gain control and make his mark as an effective ruler of the new united kingdom, James VI of Scotland (James I of England) banned weapons and established mounted forces to police the area. Reiving families – often identified with the help of local informers – were scattered and members transported or even executed.

After Archibald Armstrong of Mangerton was executed in 1610, the Armstrongs lost their lands to the Scotts, another powerful local family. However, the family didn't disappear and members of this once fearsome tribe have continued to make their mark on the world. Most famous of all must be Neil Armstrong, who carried a fragment of Armstrong tartan when he stepped on to the surface of the moon, in 1969.

Walk 6

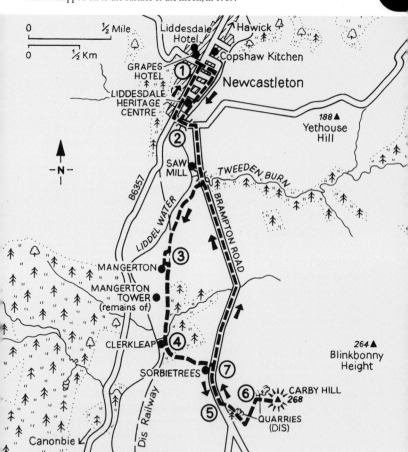

Walk 6 Directions

① From **Douglas Square**, with your back to the **Grapes Hotel**, walk along **Wyitchester Street** (or any other street opposite) and go down to the **Liddel Water**. Turn right, walk along the riverbank and join the path downstream to reach the bridge. Turn left at the top of the steps and cross the bridge.

Walk 6

② After about 100yds (91m), turn right and follow the **Brampton Road**, passing static caravans on either side. You'll eventually pass an old sawmill with a corrugated iron roof and will then reach the **Tweeden Burn bridge**. Cross the bridge and walk uphill, then turn right and join the metalled track that leads to **Mangerton farm**. Continue on this road until you near the farm buildings.

WHERE TO EAT AND DRINK ⓘ

You've got a few choices in Newcastleton. There's the **Grapes Hotel** on Douglas Square or the **Liddesdale Hotel**, also on Douglas Square, both of which serve bar meals. You can also try the **Copshaw Kitchen**, a coffee shop and licensed restaurant, which is on North Hermitage Street.

---

③ You now turn left, then sharp right, and walk down on to the bed of the old railway line, which has joined you from the right. This line once linked Carlisle to Edinburgh but was closed following the Beeching cuts of 1963. Follow the line as it leads past the remains of **Mangerton Tower**, in a field to your right, and continue until you reach **Clerkleap cottage**.

④ Turn left immediately after the cottage, then go through the

---

WHAT TO LOOK FOR ⓘ

You'll probably notice plenty of **stinging nettles** as you walk along the old railway line. That's because they love to grow on disturbed ground and flourish in environments such as this. They're a real favourite of **butterflies** such as the red admiral as they provide a juicy source of food for their caterpillars.

---

wooden gate to join a rough track. This leads through woodland and on, uphill, to join the road by **Sorbietrees farm**. Turn right now and walk along the road, past the farm, to a small stand of conifers on the left. Turn left through the gate.

⑤ Bear right now and head up the left-hand side of the trees. Walk past the top of the wood and a former quarry, to reach a dry-stone wall. Turn left and follow the wall uphill, crossing it about 437yds (400m) ahead at a convenient right-angle bend.

⑥ It's a bit of a scramble now, over bracken and scree, to reach the summit – the views are great though. Known locally as **Caerba Hill**, this was once the site of a prehistoric settlement. You now have to retrace your steps to reach the road again, then turn right and walk back to **Sorbietrees farm**.

WHILE YOU'RE THERE ⓘ

Liddesdale Heritage Centre and Museum is the place to come to learn more about the history of the area and its people. Trainspotters will love the Waverley Line memorabilia, which includes a seat from the station platform and an old railway clock. And if you're trying to trace your family tree you can make use of their genealogical records.

---

⑦ At the farm, continue on the main road as it bears right and follow it back over the **Tweeden bridge** and up to the **Holm Bridge**. Cross the bridge and walk straight on for 100yds (91m), then turn right on to the **B6357** and walk back to the village square via the little **heritage centre**.

Thirty-Nine Steps in Broughton

A lovely walk through John Buchan country.

·DISTANCE·	5 miles (8km)
·MINIMUM TIME·	2hrs 30min
·ASCENT / GRADIENT·	1,575ft (480m) ▲▲▲
·LEVEL OF DIFFICULTY·	林林 林林 林
·PATHS·	Hill tracks and grassy paths, 1 stile
·LANDSCAPE·	Rolling hills and exposed ridge
·SUGGESTED MAP·	aqua3 OS Explorer 336 Biggar & Broughton
·START / FINISH·	Grid reference: NT 119374
·DOG FRIENDLINESS·	Good, but keep on lead because of sheep
·PARKING·	Parking in front of cottage past Broughton Place Art Gallery
·PUBLIC TOILETS·	None on route

BACKGROUND TO THE WALK

I had been walking for about half an hour when I spotted a man standing alone on Broughton Heights. I thought nothing of it until he began to wave urgently. Thinking he was in some sort of trouble I climbed the hill. When I reached the top I saw that he was dressed in a tweed jacket and carried a small pack. His piercing blue eyes met mine: 'Hello Hannay,' he said holding out his hand. 'I have a message for you. We need your help.' …

Sorry, I was getting carried away there. John Buchan didn't write those words, I did, but these rugged hills around Broughton were once trodden by the author of *The Thirty-Nine Steps* and you can't help but be inspired to flights of fancy by memories of his taut tales of intrigue and derring-do. Although he was born in Perth (in 1875), Buchan has close links with this area as his grandparents lived here and he spent many summer holidays in the village. A keen hillwalker, it is almost certain that he frequently followed the same tracks that you take on this exhilarating circuit.

Buchan's most famous fictional creation is the upper-class hero Richard Hannay, who featured in the spy thriller *The Thirty-Nine Steps* (1915). But this was not his only novel. He wrote many other adventure stories (or 'shockers' as he liked to call them) – four of them featuring Richard Hannay, as well as a book of poetry and several historical works including biographies of Sir Walter Scott and Oliver Cromwell.

A Career to Envy

He was an extraordinarily successful man and must have greatly annoyed his contemporaries who could never have hoped to match his achievements. After Oxford University (where he naturally became President of the Union and gained a First), he became a barrister. During the First World War he was appointed Director of Information, and then wrote a 24-volume history of the war. In 1927 he became a Member of Parliament

Walk 7

and was made a Companion of Honour in 1932 – publishing more works all the time. As his career flourished he came into contact with many great characters, including Henry James and Lawrence of Arabia.

Buchan must have had immense energy and obviously impressed those around him, for in 1935 he was appointed Governor-General of Canada and was given a peerage – taking the title Baron Tweedsmuir of Elsfield. Tweedsmuir is a hamlet close to the village of Broughton and the area featured in a number of Buchan's works. Broughton was the village of 'Woodilee' in a little-known novel *Witch Wood* (1927), while much of the action in his adventure novels is played out on the moody moors and lonely hills of the Borders. John Buchan died in Canada in 1940. He would probably be surprised to find that his 'shockers' are still being read and enjoyed today.

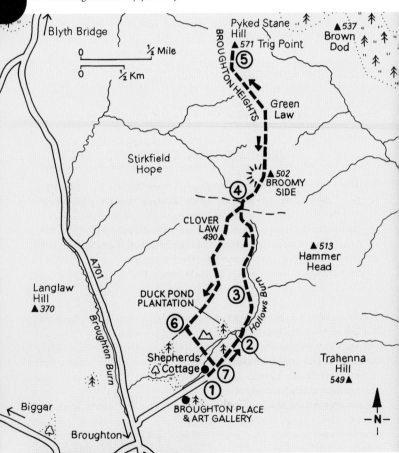

Walk 7 Directions

① From the parking place, go through the gate and follow the obvious, grassy track that runs in front of the cottage. You'll soon pass a copse on the left-hand side and will then pass the attractively named **Duck Pond Plantation**, also on the left-hand side. The track becomes slightly rougher now and you cross wooden rollers to help you over a burn.

Walk 7

② Your track continues ahead, over a larger burn and past feathery carpets of heather and bracken – listen for the skylarks in the summer. Continue walking and the path will soon level out and lead you past a deep gully on the right-hand side. Follow the track until it bends, after which you come to a meeting of tracks.

> **WHILE YOU'RE THERE** ⓘ
> If you're a real John Buchan fan you can make a pilgrimage to the **John Buchan Centre**, which is at the far end of Broughton village. It's housed in an old church where Buchan and his relatives once attended services. It's a small museum full of photographs, books and general memorabilia that illustrate the life and achievements of the author.

③ Take the track that bears left and head for the dip that lies between the two hills – **Clover Law** on the left and **Broomy Side** in front. You should just be able to spot the fence on the skyline. Make for that fence and, as you near it, you'll eventually spot a gate, next to which is a wooden stile.

④ Cross the stile, then turn right and follow the fence line. You soon get superb views to the left – well, you do on a clear day. Continue following the fence and walk up the track until you reach the trig point on **Broughton Heights** – the final ascent's a bit of a puff – but it's thankfully not too long.

⑤ Now retrace your steps to reach the stile again, nip over it, but this time turn right and follow the narrow track that climbs **Clover Law**. Continue walking in the same direction, following the fence line as it runs along the top of the ridge. When you near the end of the

> **WHERE TO EAT AND DRINK** ⓘ
> The best place for tea is the **Laurel Bank tea room**, which can be found in the centre of Broughton. It serves home-made soup and light meals such as baked potatoes and toasted sandwiches, as well as freshly baked cakes and scones. The atmosphere is friendly and they're used to walkers.

ridge, keep your eyes peeled and look for the track that leads down to your left.

⑥ Follow the track as it runs down between the two plantations, roughly in the direction of the cottage – it's quite a steep descent. At the bottom you'll come to an old wall and a burn, which you cross, then continue ahead to reach the main track.

⑦ Turn right here and walk past the little cottage again, through the gate and back to your car. If you want to visit **Broughton Place** and its art gallery, just continue walking down the track to reach the house on your left.

> **WHAT TO LOOK FOR** ⓘ
> The **Broughton Gallery** showcases the work of leading British artists and craftspeople. As well as paintings in oil and watercolour, you can find hand-made glass, ceramics, painted silk, carved wood and distinctive jewellery. The goods are for sale so you'd better bring your credit card – you might find a local landscape that you just can't resist.

A Reference to Peebles

There are reminders of the founders of an encyclopaedia on this lovely walk.

Walk 8

•DISTANCE•	3½ miles (5.7km)
•MINIMUM TIME•	1hr 20min
•ASCENT / GRADIENT•	295ft (90m) ▲▲▲
•LEVEL OF DIFFICULTY•	🏃 🏃 🏃
•PATHS•	Waymarked riverside paths and metalled tracks
•LANDSCAPE•	Rolling borderlands and Tweed Valley
•SUGGESTED MAP•	aqua3 OS Explorer 337 Peebles & Innerleithen
•START / FINISH•	Grid reference: NT 250402
•DOG FRIENDLINESS•	Great, loads of smells and chance to swim
•PARKING•	Kingsmeadows Road car park, Peebles
•PUBLIC TOILETS•	At car park

BACKGROUND TO THE WALK

Next time you're watching *University Challenge*, listening to *Brain of Britain*, or even taking part in your local pub quiz night – think for a moment about the person who has compiled the questions. They've almost certainly come up with some of them after referring to an encyclopaedia. We tend to take these great tomes for granted, casually assuming that everything they say is correct, but never giving any thought to the people that produce them. This walk will change that, as it starts and finishes in the bustling town of Peebles – the birthplace of the Chambers brothers, the founding publishers of the famous *Chambers' Encyclopaedia*.

William, the older brother, was born in 1800 and in 1814 was apprenticed to a bookseller in Edinburgh. Robert, born in 1802, later followed him to the city and in 1819 they set up in business as booksellers, then branched out into printing as well. They seemed to have a flair for the trade and, in 1832, William started *Chambers' Edinburgh Journal*, a publication to which Robert contributed many essays. It was a success and later that year the brothers established the publishing house W & R Chambers. Robert, who seemed to be the more literary of the two, continued to write in his spare time and in 1844 anonymously published a book with the less-than-catchy title *Vestiges of the Natural History of Creation*. It was a controversial work, dealing with issues that it were then considered blasphemy even to discuss. Charles Darwin later praised it, saying it had helped to prepare the ground for his book *On the Origin of Species* (1859), which outlined his revolutionary theory of evolution.

An Encyclopaedia is Born

The first edition of the *Chambers' Encyclopaedia* (1859–68) encompassed ten volumes and was edited by Robert. It was based on a translation of a German work. Robert, who had become friendly with Sir Walter Scott, continued to write, producing books on a wide range of subjects such as history, literature and geology. He also wrote a reference work entitled *A Biographical Dictionary of Eminent Scotsmen* (1832–4).

Although not as prolific as his brother, William too wrote a number of books, including a *History of Peeblesshire* , which came out in 1864. He did not forget his origins in Peebles and in 1859 he founded and endowed a museum, library and art gallery in the town. It's still there today, on the High Street, and is worth visiting, if only for an enormous frieze – a copy of the Elgin marbles that were taken from the Parthenon in Athens. When the brothers died, Robert in 1871 and William in 1883, the company was taken over by Robert's son. The name Chambers is still associated with scholarly reference works today.

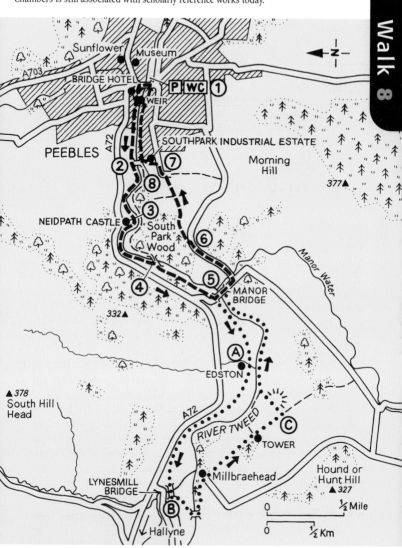

Walk 8 Directions

① From Kingsmeadows car park, turn right and cross the bridge. Turn left at the **Bridge Hotel** and walk down the slope, past the swimming pool, to the river. Cross a

small footbridge, go up some steps, turn left and follow the riverside track to pass a white bridge and a children's play area.

② Continue following the obvious path and go over a little bridge over a burn, after which the path

Walk 8

becomes a little more rugged. You now enter the woods, going through a kissing gate and following the signs for the 'Tweed Walk'. Eventually you'll leave the woods and will come to romantic-looking **Neidpath Castle** on the right-hand side.

③ From the castle continue walking by the river to go through another kissing gate. You'll soon come on to higher ground and will get a great view of the old railway bridge spanning the water in front of you. After another kissing gate, maintain your direction to reach the red sandstone bridge.

WHERE TO EAT AND DRINK ⓘ
There are plenty of places to choose from in Peebles. My favourite is **Sunflower**, a contemporary restaurant just off the main street. You can get cappuccino and a large piece of cake or choose one of their more substantial meals such as delicous bruschetta with avocado. The food's always fresh and well presented.

④ Go up to the right of the bridge, so that you join the old railway line – you now maintain direction and continue following the Tweed Walk. Follow this disused track until you reach another attractive bridge – **Manor Bridge**.

⑤ Turn left here and cross the bridge, then take the turning on the left signed 'Tweed Walk'. You're now on a metalled track that winds uphill – do stop and look behind you for classic views of the Borders landscape, with lush rolling hills and the wide, busy Tweed. Continue until you reach a track on the left that leads into the woods – it's signed 'public footpath to Peebles by Southpark'.

⑥ Follow this track for a few paces, then take the wide grassy path which you follow until you leave the wood by a ladder stile. Follow the grassy path downhill, nip over another stile and follow the enclosed path – you'll get good views of Peebles now. Follow the obvious track until you join a wide tarmac road.

WHILE YOU'RE THERE ⓘ
Neidpath Castle, which you pass on this walk, dates back to the 14th century. Its walls are 11ft (3m) thick and conceal a pit prison as well as several historic rooms. It never really saw much action, except for the time in 1650 when it was besieged by Cromwell.

⑦ Follow this road and turn left into **Southpark Industrial Estate**. Walk to the bottom right-hand corner past the units, then go down some steps and bear left when you reach the bottom. You'll soon reach a footbridge ahead of you.

⑧ Turn right here and follow the wide track beside the river. This is a popular part of the walk and attracts lots of families on sunny days. Continue walking past the weir, then go up the steps at the bridge and cross over to return to the car park.

WHAT TO LOOK FOR ⓘ
The last time I did this walk I spotted a **kingfisher** darting low over the river. These brilliantly coloured birds are expert anglers, eating fish like minnows and sticklebacks, as well as tadpoles and insects like dragonflies. The bird was called the 'halcyon' by the ancient Greeks, who said that it bred in a floating nest at sea, calming stormy weather. That's how we get the word 'halcyon' which refers to a peaceful, happy time.

Walk 9

And a Note on the Tweed

A longer walk along the banks of the Tweed.
See map and information panel for Walk 8

•DISTANCE•	3½ miles (5.7km)
•MINIMUM TIME•	1hr 30min
•ASCENT / GRADIENT•	66ft (20m) ▲▲ ▲ ▲
•LEVEL OF DIFFICULTY•	🚶🚶 🚶 🚶

Walk 9 Directions (Walk 8 option)

At Point ⑤ on the walk, don't turn left across the bridge but simply cross to the other side, nip over the stile and go up some steps to rejoin the old railway line. It's easy going and you just follow the path which is laced with hawthorn, birch and willow trees, as well as brambles, nettles, wild roses and gorse. Eventually you'll pass **Edston farm** (Point Ⓐ) on the right-hand side and might have to cross a couple of stiles on the track (if the gates aren't opened).

The track now takes you further from the river and is full of wild flowers in the spring and summer. Cross another couple of stiles and follow the track as it narrows, then eventually opens out into pasture. You'll pass a small house over to the right and will then see lovely old **Lynesmill Bridge**, also on the right.

Your route now takes you over an old railway bridge. Turn left at the end (Point Ⓑ) and go down the steps, then turn right at the bottom and walk along the metalled road, passing a few houses on either side. Then leave the road, taking the path

that runs to the right of the fence in front and cross the river by the metal bridge. Follow the enclosed track into woodland and, at the fingerpost, bear right, following the Tweed Walk signs. Your track is wide now and leads you past the front of a little house on the left-hand side.

Maintain your direction down the long straight avenue marked 'Private Road to Barns'. Turn right at the pink tower and walk along the track, before turning left at the fingerpost (Point Ⓒ). You get great views of the hills now and will soon come to a small valley. Cross a couple of stiles and walk down to the river, then bear right following the obvious track by the riverside. Your way now takes you over a ladder stile and then two more stiles until you reach **Manor Bridge**. Take the steps up on to the bridge then turn right and rejoin Walk 8 at Point ⑤.

WHAT TO LOOK FOR ⓘ

The **Tweed** is a lovely river that has inspired many artists and writers. Described by Sir Walter Scott as 'broad and deep', the river is a favourite haunt of fishermen as it contains salmon. Its source is near Moffat in the south west and it then snakes its way across Scotland to Berwick-upon-Tweed.

Walk 10

Utopia at New Lanark

A rustic walk from a model industrial community.

•DISTANCE•	6 miles (9.7km)
•MINIMUM TIME•	3hrs
•ASCENT / GRADIENT•	476ft (145m) ▲▲▲
•LEVEL OF DIFFICULTY•	👥 👥 👥
•PATHS•	Clear riverside tracks and forest paths, few steep steps
•LANDSCAPE•	Planned industrial town and some stunning waterfalls
•SUGGESTED MAP•	aqua3 OS Explorer 335 Lanark & Tinto Hills
•START / FINISH•	Grid reference: NS 883425
•DOG FRIENDLINESS•	Good, plenty of smells by river and can mostly run free
•PARKING•	Main car park above New Lanark
•PUBLIC TOILETS•	Visitor centre (when open)

Walk 10 Directions

From the car park, walk downhill. You'll soon see the mills below you. Walk past the church and into the centre of the planned industrial village of New Lanark. This was built as a cotton-spinning centre in 1785 and is so well preserved that it is now a UNESCO World Heritage Site. It owes its fame to Welshman Robert Owen, who took over its management in 1799 and made it the focus of a revolutionary social experiment. Unlike most industrialists of his day, Owen did not allow children under ten to work in his mills – he established the world's first nursery school and ensured that all children received a rounded initial education. He disapproved of cruel treatment of his workers and refused to allow corporal punishment to be used as a form of discipline. His workers were provided with good housing, free medical care and their own co-operative store. Although Owen couldn't create Utopia, he did inspire the creation of several other model villages such as Saltaire, Port Sunlight and Bournville.

Bear left now and follow the signs to the Scottish Wildlife Trust centre. Now turn up the stone steps on the left, following the signs to the **Falls of Clyde**. Follow the path, then go down some steps to reach the weir, where there's a lookout point. Now continue to follow the path. You'll eventually pass **Bonnington Power Station** on your right, where the path divides. Take the right-hand path, which begins to climb and takes you into woodland and up some steps. You'll soon come to **Corra Linn waterfall**, where there's another lookout point. There's a

---

WHILE YOU'RE THERE ⓘ

The ruins of Corra Castle, built in the 13th century, are home to a colony of **Natterer's bat**. These medium-sized bats are found throughout Britain. In winter they tend to hibernate in caves and mines, while in summer they prefer to roost in old stone buildings and barns. Their limbs have a slight pink tinge, giving rise to the bats' nickname of the 'red-armed bat'.

plaque here explaining how the falls inspired painters such as Turner and Moore, as well as the poet Wordsworth, who visited the falls in 1802 with his sister Dorothy and friend Samuel Taylor Coleridge. Your path then continues to the right, signposted 'Bonnington Linn ¾ mile'.

Go up some more steps and follow the wide track until you go under a double line of pylons. Just after this is an area that is often fenced off to protect breeding peregrines – their nest site is surveyed by cameras until the young have left the nest. The path is obvious though so you can't go wrong – and you follow it until you reach the large new bridge. Cross over the bridge, then turn right into the **Falls of Clyde Wildlife Reserve**. Walk through the reserve until you come to a crossing of paths at which you turn right, then walk over a small bridge. Walk underneath the double line of pylons again, then bear right at the gate.

> ### WHERE TO EAT AND DRINK
> There's a self-service **café** in the village where you can get baked potatoes with various fillings, sandwiches, cakes and hot drinks. On fine days you can buy ice creams from a **kiosk** in the village and you can also buy tooth-rotting fudge from the old-fashioned **village store**.

You'll come to **Corra Castle**, hidden away on the right-hand side. It's very atmospheric and overgrown with ivy – but you mustn't go in as you could disturb the bats (▶ While You're There). Now continue walking by the river, go over a small footbridge then follow the wide path that leads through the woods. When you meet another path, turn right and you'll soon come to some houses on your left-hand side. When you reach the road turn right (take care as there's no pavement), then go right again to walk over the old bridge. This brings you into a cul de sac, where you go through the gate on the right-hand side – it looks as if you are going into someone's drive but it's signed 'Clyde Walkway'.

Walk past the stables and down to the river. Go through a metal gate to reach a **water treatment works** and walk up the steps beside it. Walk past a stile on your left and continue on the main track, following the signs for the Clyde Walkway. Pass a house on the right-hand side, then follow the path that leads down to the right (there's a fingerpost but the finger had been broken off when I was there). Your path now zig-zags downhill to reach the river. When you come to the water's edge turn left, go over a footbridge and follow the wide forest track. You'll go down some steps, close to the river again, then up a flight of stairs and over a bridge. Just after this you'll get some great views of the mills again. Follow the path as it winds back on to the road, then turn right and walk down the hill and back into **New Lanark**. Turn left at the church and walk back to the car park.

> ### WHAT TO LOOK FOR
> **Peregrines** nest near the Corra Linn Falls from April to June and high-powered telescopes have been set up to allow you to view their nest without disturbing the birds. They are a protected species and there are only around 800 pairs in Scotland. Sadly, they are threatened by egg collectors, shooting and poisoning. Peregrines are noted for their steep dive to catch their prey, at speeds of up to 120mph (193kph).

Remembering the Jacobites at Traquair

You'll find Jacobite connections in an atmospheric old house and a moorland fairy well, on this walk.

•DISTANCE•	6½ miles (10.4km)
•MINIMUM TIME•	2hrs 45min
•ASCENT / GRADIENT•	1,378ft (420m) ▲▲▲
•LEVEL OF DIFFICULTY•	🚶🚶 🚶🚶 🚶🚶
•PATHS•	Firm, wide moorland tracks, 1 stile
•LANDSCAPE•	Rolling hills and heather-clad moors – some excellent views
•SUGGESTED MAP•	aqua3 OS Explorer 337 Peebles & Innerleithen
•START / FINISH•	Grid reference: NT 331345
•DOG FRIENDLINESS•	Can run free for long stretches – but on lead near sheep
•PARKING•	Southern Upland Way car park in Traquair
•PUBLIC TOILETS•	None on route; nearest in car park at Peebles

BACKGROUND TO THE WALK

There can be few more romantic places in Britain than Traquair House, which is just a couple of minutes' drive from the start of this walk. It's the oldest continually inhabited house in Scotland and is still owned by the Maxwell Stuart family, who came here in 1491. Parts of the house date back to the 12th century, although most of the present building was built in 1680. It's a house full of secret stairways and little windows and even has its own brewery, the origins of which stretch back to the 16th century. Traquair House is one of those marvellous places that simply ooze atmosphere – largely, I think, because it is still a family home.

All in a Good Cause

The house was always a popular stopping-off point for Scottish monarchs and 27 of them visited over the years, including Mary, Queen of Scots, who stayed here with her husband Darnley in 1566. The family were traditionally staunch Catholics and when the Protestant William of Orange took the throne in 1689, they joined many others in supporting the Jacobite cause. This demanded that the Stuart King James II (Charles II's brother) be reinstated on the throne and, contrary to popular myth, attracted support among English people as well as Scots. Years of repression and bloodshed followed.

Hiding Out at Traquair

The Jacobite Rebellion eventually culminated in the disastrous defeat at Culloden in 1746. You can, of course, visit the site of the battle itself, but it is somehow easier to understand what it must have been like to live during those times when you see the secret priest's room at Traquair. Often called 'priest's holes', these rooms were made in many of the great houses throughout Britain, allowing priests to live in hiding and take Mass for the devout family. The one in Traquair has such a strong atmosphere that it almost feels as if the priest has just stepped out for a moment.

Walk 11

An Aristocratic Maid

The 4th Earl of Traquair was imprisoned in the Tower of London and sentenced to death for his part in one of the early Jacobite risings. However, he managed to make a story-book escape, when his wife smuggled him out of prison by dressing him as a maid. The cloak he used as his disguise is on display at Traquair. Years later, the 5th Earl was also held prisoner in the Tower for supporting the Jacobites at Culloden.

Bonnie Prince Charlie visited Traquair in 1745, passing through the great Bear Gates – so named because of the bear statues that top the gate posts. When the prince left, the 5th Earl wished him a safe journey, closed the gates behind him and promised that they would not be opened again until there was a Stuart monarch on the throne. The gates have remained unopened ever since.

Walk 11 Directions

① From the Southern Upland Way car park, join the tarmac road and walk left away from Traquair village. Continue ahead, passing a house called **The Riggs**, and join the gravel track following signs for the Minch Moor. After you go through a kissing gate the track becomes even grassier, then you hop over a stile and enter Forestry Commission land.

② Continue on the obvious track to pass a **bothy** on the right. When you come to a crossing of tracks maintain direction, crossing an area that has been clear felled. Your route then takes you through a gate, just to the right of a cycle way. It then winds uphill, through a kissing gate, and joins up with the cycle way again.

WHERE TO EAT AND DRINK ℹ️
In Innerleithen you can get a drink at the **Traquair Arms Hotel**. They also do cakes and hot drinks, as well as more substantial meals such as filo parcels, pasta bakes and aubergine cannelloni. There's also a restaurant at **Traquair House**, as well as a Brewery Shop selling Traquair Jacobite Ale to take home.

---

③ Maintain direction, enjoying great views over Walkerburn to the left. It feels wilder and windier up here, with large tracts of heather-covered moorland by your path. When you reach a marker post, turn right and walk up to the cairn on the **Minch Moor** – the views should be great on a clear day.

④ From the cairn, retrace your steps back to the main track. Then turn left and walk back downhill – stopping to leave some food when you pass the **Cheese Well** (➤ What

---

WHAT TO LOOK FOR ℹ️
Do keep a look out for the **Cheese Well** by the burn on your way up to the moor. It's a local tradition to leave small pieces of cheese here for the fairies, in order to ensure a safe journey. I didn't have any cheese so I put out a piece of flapjack instead – I didn't want to offend them by leaving nothing!

WHILE YOU'RE THERE ℹ️
The mineral waters at **St Ronan's Well** near Innerleithen have been attracting visitors since the 18th century and inspired the eponymous novel by Sir Walter Scott. The well is covered by a pavilion and you can still sample the waters. Guided walks around the well and garden are available on request.

---

to Look For) on the left – it's by the boggy part of the path. Continue, to go through the gate again, until you reach the next crossing of tracks.

⑤ Turn left now and walk downhill. The landscape soon opens out on the right-hand side giving you pleasant views of the valley and the river winding away. When you reach the apex of a bend, turn right along the grassy track. Follow this as it bears downhill, go through a gate and walk in front of **Camp Shiel** cottage.

⑥ Go through another gate, cross the burn, then follow the grassy track and pass **Damhead Shiel** cottage. Go through another gate and follow the path across a bridge over a burn. You'll pass an expanse of scree on the right-hand side, and an ox-bow lake evolving on the left. Cross another bridge and continue to **Damhead farm**.

⑦ Walk past the farm and down to the road, then turn right. You'll now cross the burn again and will walk past some cottages on the right-hand side. When you reach the **war memorial** on the left, turn right and walk up the track to reach the parking place at the start of the walk on the left.

Holy Orders at Jedburgh

Follow waymarked footpaths from this historic town.

·DISTANCE·	4½ miles (7.2km)
·MINIMUM TIME·	3hrs
·ASCENT / GRADIENT·	295ft (90m) ▲▲▲
·LEVEL OF DIFFICULTY·	🚶 🚶 🚶
·PATHS·	Tracks, meadow paths and some sections of road, 2 stiles
·LANDSCAPE·	Gentle hills and fine old abbey
·SUGGESTED MAP·	aqua3 OS Explorer OL16 The Cheviot Hills
·START / FINISH·	Grid reference: NT 651204
·DOG FRIENDLINESS·	Fair, but keep on lead near sheep and on road
·PARKING·	Main car park by tourist information centre
·PUBLIC TOILETS·	At car park

BACKGROUND TO THE WALK

Although it was built back in the 12th century, the beauty and grandeur of Jedburgh Abbey is still clearly evident. It certainly dominates this bustling border town, and sits serene and seemingly untroubled by the hustle and hassle of modern life. It must have seemed still more impressive in medieval times, when the power of the Church was at its height and the population was generally uneducated and superstitious.

The abbey is one of four in the Borders – the others being at Dryburgh, Kelso and Melrose – and all were built after the Norman Conquest. They are stretched across the Borders like a string of ecclesiastical jewels. Jedburgh Abbey is one of the most impressive medieval buildings in Scotland. It was built for French Augustinian canons in 1138 by David I, on the site of an earlier Anglo-Saxon monastery, and was specifically designed to make a visual impact. This was not because the King was exceedingly devout, but was owing to the fact that Jedburgh is very close to the border with England. David needed to make an obvious statement of authority to his powerful Norman neighbours.

Monastic Life

Each of the Border abbeys belonged to a different religious order. The Augustinian canons at Jedburgh were also known as 'Black Canons' owing to the colour of their robes. Unlike monks, canons were all ordained clergymen who were allowed to administer Holy Communion. Dryburgh Abbey was founded by Premonstratensian (try saying that when you've had a few refreshments) canons, who wore white robes and lived a more secluded life than the Augustinians. Kelso Abbey, which became one of the largest monasteries in Scotland, belonged to the Benedictine order, while Melrose was founded by Cistercian monks. The Cistercians took their name from the forest of Cîteaux in France, where their first community was established. Often known as 'White Benedictines', Cistercian monks adhered strictly to the Rule of St Benedict. Manual labour in the abbey was carried out by poor, and generally illiterate, lay brothers. These people lived and worshipped separately to the 'choir' monks who devoted their time to reading, writing and private prayer. The Cistercians adhered to a strict regime, designed to purify their lives. They banned the use of bedspreads, combs and even underwear.

Abbeys Under Fire

These medieval abbeys all suffered in the battles that ravaged the Borders for centuries. Jedburgh, for example, was stripped of its roofing lead by Edward I's troops who stayed here during the Wars of Independence. It came under attack many times and was burned by the Earl of Surrey in 1530. After the Reformation, all the abbeys fell into decline and began to decay. Today they remain picturesque reminders of a previous age.

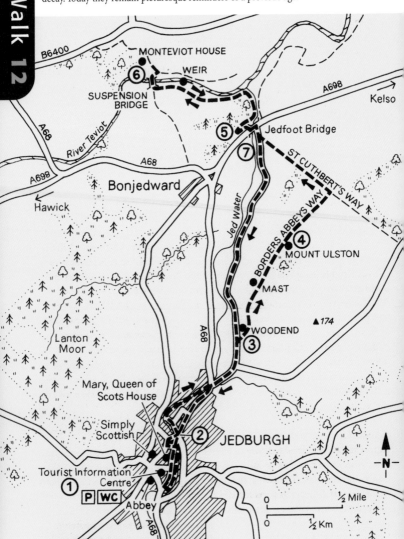

Walk 12 Directions

① From the car park, walk back to the **A68**. Turn right, then cross over before you reach the river. Take the

path on the left to walk beside the river, under an old bridge, then come on to the road. Cross and join the road opposite. Take the first right turn, then turn right at the **fire station** and cross the bridge.

② Turn left, following the sign for the Borders Abbeys Way. Where the road divides, turn left and walk beside the river again – there's a small 'W' waymarker. When you reach the main road, cross over and walk along the tarmac road. Keep going until you reach a large building on your left (it was derelict at the time of writing).

> **WHILE YOU'RE THERE** ℹ
> In the town centre you can visit **Mary, Queen of Scots House**, a 16th-century fortified house where she stayed while visiting Jedburgh in 1566. She stayed here for several weeks recovering from a severe illness, caught following a lengthy moorland ride to Hermitage Castle, where she went to visit her injured lover, the Earl of Bothwell. Years later she regretted the fact that she hadn't died in Jedburgh.

③ Turn right here to walk in front of a small farmhouse called **Woodend**. When you reach another tarmac road, turn left. Your route now runs uphill, taking you past a radio mast and in front of **Mount Ulston house**. Maintain direction to join the narrow grassy track – this can get very muddy, even in the summer.

④ Squelch along this track until you reach the fingerpost at the end, where you turn left to join **St Cuthbert's Way**. The going becomes much easier now as it's a wide, firm track. When you reach

> **WHERE TO EAT AND DRINK** ℹ
> **Simply Scottish** on the High Street in Jedburgh is a good licensed bistro with cheery yellow walls, pine tables and wooden floors. As well as serving lunches such as ploughman's, it also serves fresh scones, hearty breakfasts and more substantial meals in the evening.

the tarmac road, turn right and join the main road. Turn left, go over the bridge, then cross the road and go down some steps to continue following St Cuthbert's Way.

⑤ You're now on a narrow, grassy track which runs beside the river. You then have to nip over a couple of stiles, before walking across a meadow frequently grazed by sheep. Walk past the weir, then go through the gate to cross the suspension bridge – take care as it can get extremely slippery.

⑥ You now pass a sign for **Monteviot House** and walk through the woods to reach a fingerpost, where you can turn right to enjoy views over the river. If you wish to extend your walk, you can continue along St Cuthbert's Way until it joins the road, then retrace your steps. Whatever you choose, you then retrace your steps back over the suspension bridge, along the riverside and back to the main road. Cross over and rejoin the tarmac track.

> **WHAT TO LOOK FOR** ℹ
> **Monteviot House Gardens** are open to the public from around April to October. There's a River Garden, with views over the Teviot; a walled Rose Garden, a Herb Garden and a Water Garden made of islands which are linked by bridges. If it's raining you can always take shelter in the large greenhouse.

⑦ The track almost immediately forks and you now turn right, following the road all the way back to join the **A68** once again. When you reach the road, turn left and follow it back into **Jedburgh**. Eventually you'll come to the car park on the left-hand side, which was the starting point of the walk.

Walk 13

One of Scotland's Great Scotts at Dryburgh

A gentle walk in the Borders countryside that was much beloved by that great national figure, Sir Walter Scott.

•DISTANCE•	4½ miles (7.2km)
•MINIMUM TIME•	1hr 30min
•ASCENT / GRADIENT•	131ft (40m) ▲ ▲ ▲
•LEVEL OF DIFFICULTY•	栋栋 栋 栋
•PATHS•	Firm woodland and riverside tracks, 3 stiles
•LANDSCAPE•	Historic abbey and riverbanks
•SUGGESTED MAP•	aqua3 OS Explorer 338 Galashiels, Selkirk & Melrose
•START / FINISH•	Grid reference: NT 592318
•DOG FRIENDLINESS•	Keep on lead on Mertoun Estate and by golf course
•PARKING•	Dryburgh Abbey car park
•PUBLIC TOILETS•	At car park

BACKGROUND TO THE WALK

Walk anywhere in the Borders and you are probably following in the footsteps of one of Scotland's most celebrated literary figures – Sir Walter Scott. He travelled widely here and was celebrated during his lifetime, writing books that would be described as bestsellers if they were published today. Yet, while everyone has heard of Sir Walter Scott, hardly anyone now reads his books.

Wavering over *Waverley*
The reason for this is almost certainly the somewhat impenetrable nature of the language he uses – impenetrable to non Scots, anyway. Full of enthusiasm, people tend to pick up a copy of *Waverley* (1814), a romantic tale of the Jacobite rebellion, then put it down in defeat after page ten. But those that persist and learn to unravel the old Scots dialect discover tales that were strongly influenced by the ballads, folklore and history of the borderlands – tales that would have died out otherwise.

From Polio to Poetry
Scott was the son of an Edinburgh lawyer but spent a lot of time in the Borders as a child while recuperating from polio. He was fascinated by the stories and ballads he heard and, when he grew older, began to collect material that he later turned into romantic poetry. He was greatly influenced by Robert Burns and became friends with James Hogg, the Ettrick Shepherd (► Walk 2). Scott became a barrister in 1792, but spent his spare time writing poetry. He was appointed Sheriff-Depute of Selkirk in 1799 and in 1811 he moved to Abbotsford, a farmhouse near Melrose, where he lived for the rest of his life. He turned to novel-writing, declaring that 'Byron beat me' at poetry.

It was a decision that was to make Scott's fortune – but it was also, ultimately, to cost him his health. After the publication of *Waverley*, he produced several more historical novels, including *Rob Roy* (1817), *The Heart of Midlothian* (1818) and *Ivanhoe* (1819).

Doing the Honours

Scott didn't just write about Scottish history, however – he also played his part in it. His novels revived interest in Scottish culture, at a time when it had been in danger of disappearing. In 1818 he discovered the Honours of Scotland, a crown, sword and sceptre, which had been hidden in Edinburgh Castle from the time of Charles II (➤ Walk 50). And a few years later he was invited to make the arrangements for George IV's visit to Scotland – the King entered wholeheartedly into the spirit of the visit and delighted the crowds by wearing a kilt teamed with some natty pink tights.

Scott should have been able to relax and live in comfort, but in 1825 his publishing house collapsed and he was left with enormous debts. His wife died the same year. Scott worked furiously to pay off his debts, but his health suffered and in 1832 he died at Abbotsford. He is buried in the ruins of Dryburgh Abbey.

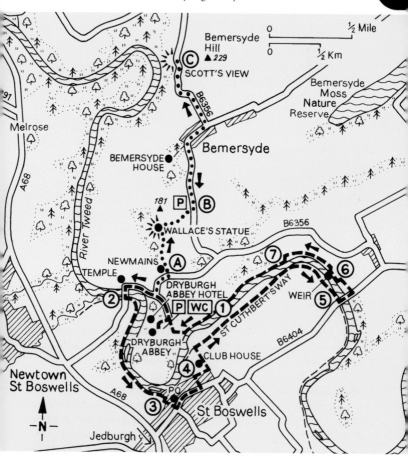

Walk 13 Directions

① From the car park at the abbey walk back to join the road, pass the entrance to the **Dryburgh Abbey Hotel**, then walk down the road in front of you. You'll soon see the river and will then pass a small temple in the trees on the right-hand side. Go left and cross the bridge over the **River Tweed**.

Walk 13

② Turn left immediately and join the **St Cuthbert's Way**. This waymarked trail now takes you along the banks of the river. At some points there are steps, tiny footbridges and patches of boardwalk to assist you. Continue to follow this trail which eventually takes you past two small islands in the river, where it then leads away from the riverbank.

③ Follow the trail on to a tarmac track, bear right and then left. At the main road in **St Boswells** go left again and continue to follow the trail signs, passing a **post office** and later Scott's View chippy on your left. After house No 101, turn left then go to your right along a tarmac track at the end.

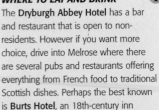

WHILE YOU'RE THERE

Abbotsford, west of Melrose, was Sir Walter Scott's home from 1811 until his death. He spent an enormous amount of money turning the original farmhouse into the home you see today. Scott's influence can be felt everywhere, from the library, which contains over 9,000 rare books, to the historic relics, such as Rob Roy's gun. You can visit both the house and grounds and there's a handy tea room too.

④ Follow this, then turn left and walk past the golf club house. Continue walking for a few paces, then turn right and follow the St Cuthbert's Way as it hugs the golf course. You now continue by the golf course until your track

eventually brings you back down to the riverbank. Walk past the weir and up to the bridge.

⑤ Go up the steps and cross the bridge, then turn sharp left and walk towards the cottages. Before the cottages, go left, over the footbridge, then turn right along the riverbank to walk in front of them. At the weir, take the steps that run up to the right, nip over the stile and into a field.

WHERE TO EAT AND DRINK

The **Dryburgh Abbey Hotel** has a bar and restaurant that is open to non-residents. However if you want more choice, drive into Melrose where there are several pubs and restaurants offering everything from French food to traditional Scottish dishes. Perhaps the best known is **Burts Hotel**, an 18th-century inn which serves good bar meals and offers a choice of 50 single malt whiskies.

⑥ Go left now, through the gate, and follow the indistinct track – it's overgrown with high grasses in the summer but isn't hard to follow. Where the path divides, go left to keep to the river – you'll now be on short, springy grass.

⑦ Follow the river, keeping an eye out for fish leaping up to feed from the water's surface. You'll cross a stile, then pass a greenhouse on your left. Climb another stile here, turn right, walk past the toilets and, at the house ahead, turn left and walk back into the car park.

WHAT TO LOOK FOR

The nearby Eildon Hills are a favourite haunt of **buzzards**. The common buzzard is Britain's most numerous large bird of prey and feeds on rabbits and other small mammals. It's had a chequered history and was badly affected by the introduction of myxomatosis in the mid-1950s, which almost obliterated the rabbit population. Sadly buzzards are still often killed by poisoned food that farmers and gamekeepers put out to kill foxes and crows.

Walk 14

A Diversion to Scott's View

A linear walk to see the Eildon Hills from Sir Walter Scott's favourite spot.
See map and information panel for Walk 13

•DISTANCE•	3½ miles (5.7km)
•MINIMUM TIME•	1hr
•ASCENT / GRADIENT•	394ft (120m) ▲▲▲
•LEVEL OF DIFFICULTY•	🚶🚶🚶

Walk 14 Directions (Walk 13 option)

You can do this extension at either the beginning or the end of the walk. From the parking place in Dryburgh (Point ① on the main walk) walk back to join the road, pass the entrance to the **Dryburgh Abbey Hotel** and follow the main road as it bends round. Just past the house called **Newmains** (Point Ⓐ), turn left and follow the public footpath uphill. It's a firm path and will eventually bring you up to the statue of William Wallace.

The statue is enormous and made of red sandstone. It's inscribed with the words 'Great Patriot Hero'. It's worth bringing your camera with you as the views from this spot on a clear day are great. Walk in front of the statue and continue to follow the path as it runs downhill. It is a clear, wide track from now and brings you down to a small car park (Point Ⓑ). Turn left now and walk along the main road.

Eventually you'll pass the entrance to **Bemersyde House and Gardens**, once the home of Earl Haig. Continue on the main road as it bears right and then left until you finally reach the wide lay-by that marks **Scott's View** (Point Ⓒ). There's a geographical indicator here pointing out places of interest. The view is great and you can see the Eildon Hills that so inspired Sir Walter Scott. Scott played a large part in encouraging a love of wild landscapes by immortalising them in his works.

To return, you retrace your steps and return to the car park, where you can rejoin the main walk at Point ①.

WHILE YOU'RE THERE

Dryburgh Abbey, set on the banks of the Tweed, is the most romantic of all the Border abbeys and simply begs to have its picture taken. It is hardly surprising that it was chosen as the burial place for Sir Walter Scott. However, few people are aware that a rather less celebrated Scot is buried here – Field Marshal Earl Haig. Haig was the commander of the British Army in the First World War and his tactics are now widely considered to have cost the lives of thousands of soldiers. The attitude to him is best summed up by Siegfried Sassoon's poem *The General*, which begins: '"Good-morning; good-morning!" the General said / When we met him last week on our way to the Line / Now the soldiers he smiled at are most of 'em dead / And we're cursing his staff for incompetent swine...'

Walk 15

A March Around the Marches of Lauder

A short but exhilarating walk in open country surrounding the historic town of Lauder, where an ancient tradition is observed each year.

•DISTANCE•	4 miles (6.4km)
•MINIMUM TIME•	1hr 30min
•ASCENT / GRADIENT•	525ft (160m) ▲▲▲
•LEVEL OF DIFFICULTY•	👫 👫 👫
•PATHS•	Grassy tracks, open fields, some overgrown rough ground
•LANDSCAPE•	Rolling hills and farmland
•SUGGESTED MAP•	aqua3 OS Explorer 338 Galashiels, Selkirk & Melrose
•START / FINISH•	Grid reference: NT 531475
•DOG FRIENDLINESS•	Keep on lead near livestock – overgrown areas and fences might be hard to negotiate
•PARKING•	High Street in Lauder
•PUBLIC TOILETS•	By Market Place in Lauder

Walk 15 Directions

Like all towns in the Borders, Lauder is steeped in tradition. The town dates back to the 12th century and the Scottish Parliament met here many times. The first Tolbooth in the Market Place, for instance, was built in 1318 so that tolls could be collected from people passing through town. However, it is more noted for its associations with witchcraft, as the ground floor was used as a jail until 1843 and witches were said to have been burned at

---

WHERE TO EAT AND DRINK ℹ

The **Flat Cat Gallery and Coffee Shop** is light and bright. On the other side of the road is the **Eagle Hotel**, which serves bar meals at lunchtime and from 6–9PM. You can choose from starters like deep-fried Camembert, and main courses like chicken breasts – there are also several veggie choices. For something special, try the **Lauderdale Hotel**.

---

the stake here. Place names such as Dunking Pool near the town are reminders that witches were often tried by being tied up and dunked into deep water. If they drowned they were considered innocent – if they survived they were guilty and burned at the stake.

From the **Market Place**, walk east to turn down **Mill Wynd** (it's by the church). Walk past the new housing estate, then bear right at the fingerpost by the car park and join the Southern Upland Way. This waymarked walk was Britain's first coast-to-coast footpath and runs for 212 miles (341km) from Portpatrick in the south west to Cockburnspath in the east. It's quite a challenging walk, with some long and demanding stretches.

The wide, grassy track now leads gently uphill, past a mobile phone mast and up to a gate. Go through the gate, ignore the path bearing

Walk 15

WHILE YOU'RE THERE ⓘ

Thirlestane Castle is more of a house than a castle and is one of the oldest stately homes in Scotland. It's the seat of the Earls of Lauderdale and has been home to the Maitland family since the 16th century. It's noted for its fine plaster ceilings, though if you've got the kids with you they'll be more interested in the collection of historic toys.

left, and continue ahead. The path is clear and firm underfoot and you're now walking with a golf course on your left and a deep river gully on your right – which looks really splendid in the setting sun.

You soon pass a small copse on the left-hand side. Continue walking past the copse and maintain direction until you start to descend towards a ladder stile. Don't cross this stile but bear to the right, leaving the Southern Upland Way. A narrow track here goes downhill at the far end of the gully. You'll soon see a distinct point where three burns meet. Cross the water here – it's not wide and there are plenty of stones to help you. You now join the obvious, narrow track that runs uphill, walking under a line of electric cables (no, not the pylons – you don't want to go as far as that).

This is lovely open countryside and it's easy to imagine people galloping past on horses. Lauder, like all the Border towns, has a Common Riding every year. Also known as the Riding of the Marches (boundaries), this is an ancient ritual that dates back to the Middle Ages when men would ride out to 'beat the bounds', re-establishing the town's boundaries and protecting common land. Today the event involves hundreds of riders who gallop wildly across the

countryside following the 'Cornet' who carries the town's standard. Lauder's Common Riding takes place early in August.

You then bear right and join another track that leads to a small **copse**. Walk past the copse, then start to bear gently round to your left to reach a wall. Cross the wall, then bear right, heading for the left-hand corner of the rectangular copse below. You'll need to climb a couple of fences now and walk across fields (which often contain livestock, so put the dog on a lead).

Your way then skirts the left edge of the copse and over a fence to reach a rusty old **Nissen hut**. With the Nissen hut on your left (it's extremely overgrown here so you'll have to negotiate some nettles), maintain your direction to join a fenced track. In summer this too is overgrown, with willowherb so high that it towers above you – however, there's only one way to go so you can't go wrong.

Eventually you'll come out by a factory farm, where you join the road. At the road turn right, walking past houses and a bowling green. When you reach the junction (you'll see the **Lauderdale Hotel** in front of you), turn right and make your way along Lauder's **High Street** and back to the start.

WHAT TO LOOK FOR ⓘ

There's plenty of **rosebay willowherb** at the end of this walk. It's a fast-spreading weed with distinctive bright pink flowers, and is found all over the British Isles. It flowers between June and September. Rosebay willowherb likes to grow on ground that has been disturbed or burned – a fact that has given it the nickname 'fireweed'.

The Gypsy Palace of Kirk Yetholm

This energetic walk takes you over the border to England.

•DISTANCE•	5 miles (8km)
•MINIMUM TIME•	3hrs 45min
•ASCENT / GRADIENT•	1,378ft (420m) ▲▲▲
•LEVEL OF DIFFICULTY•	👫 👫 👫
•PATHS•	Wide tracks and waymarked paths, one short overgrown section, 3 stiles
•LANDSCAPE•	Rolling open hills with panoramic views
•SUGGESTED MAP•	aqua3 OS Explorer OL16 The Cheviot Hills
•START / FINISH•	Grid reference: NT 839276
•DOG FRIENDLINESS•	Excellent, though keep on lead near sheep
•PARKING•	Car park outside Kirk Yetholm at junction of Pennine Way and St Cuthbert's Way
•PUBLIC TOILETS•	None on route

BACKGROUND TO THE WALK

This is such a lovely walk that I could do it again and again. It's easy to follow, the paths are good and the views have a definite 'wow' factor – so do try and save it for a clear day so that you get the full effect. The walk includes the added thrill of crossing the border from Scotland into England – no, you won't need your passport.

The little village of Kirk Yetholm was noted as a gypsy settlement from at least 1695, although they were probably there before that, as gypsies were in Scotland by the early 16th century. Gypsies were generally regarded with suspicion as they had a reputation for stealing and aggression – it was even said that they kidnapped children and brought them up as their own. However, they were also said to be loyal to those that helped them and never broke their word.

A Royal Family Home

No one is quite sure how the gypsies came to settle in Kirk Yetholm, although many moved to the wild areas of the Borders where they could hide in the hills, after a law was passed in Scotland in 1609 making it legal to kill them. Some say that a young gypsy boy saved the life of a local laird, who showed his thanks by building several homes for gypsies in the village; others, that a gypsy boy helped a local laird to recover a horse that had been stolen and was rewarded with a house in Kirk Yetholm. There were certainly several homes for gypsies in the village, with one cottage being specially built for the royal family – it's called the Gypsy Palace today.

The gypsy royal family had the surname Faa. The first king in Kirk Yetholm was Patrick Faa, who was married to Jean Gordon. Jean was born not far from here and was a powerful character who lived a wild life. Three of her sons were hanged for sheep stealing and she was eventually banned from Kirk Yetholm after attacking another woman. She was said to be the inspiration for Sir Walter Scott's gypsy character, Meg Merrilees. She was later immortalised by Keats in his eponymous poem that began: 'Old Meg she was a gypsy; and lived upon the moors: her bed it was the brown heath turf, and her house was out of doors…'.

The last queen of the gypsies was Esther Faa-Blythe who once said the scattered village was 'sae mingle-mangle that ane micht think it was either built on a dark nicht, or sawn on a windy ane'. Her son, Charles Blythe, was crowned king in 1898 – but the gypsy way of life had gone by then. Today only the Palace remains.

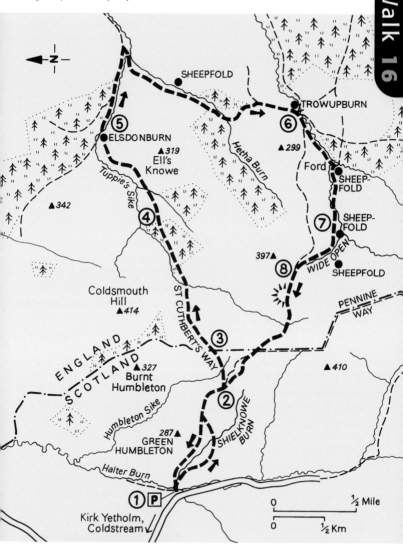

Walk 16 Directions

① From the car park cross the burn by the bridge, following the signs to the St Cuthbert's Way. Follow the

obvious track uphill, keeping the **Shielknowe Burn** below on your left. Eventually the track crosses the burn, then continues uphill, skirting the edge of **Green Humbleton hill** and eventually reaching a fingerpost.

② This is where the St Cuthbert's Way splits from the Pennine Way. Take the left-hand track, to follow the **St Cuthbert's Way**, a narrow grassy sheep track at this point. Continue following this track as it winds uphill, then takes you to a fingerpost by a wall marking the **border** between Scotland and England.

③ Follow the track which eventually bears downhill to a boggy area. Look out for the waymarkers, then continue to reach a wood. Go over the stile and into the trees. Maintain direction, then turn right at the fence and follow the fence line. You'll soon walk down an avenue of trees and leave the wood by another stile.

> ### WHERE TO EAT AND DRINK 🛈
> The **Border Hotel** in Kirk Yetholm is a friendly little pub that sits right at the end of the Pennine Way. If you want to eat there in the evening, try and book as they can get very busy.

④ Maintain your direction now across the field, then walk down to cross the burn and join a wider track. Eventually this winds down to reach **Elsdonburn farm**. Walk through the farm buildings and follow the track as it bears to the right. Join the metalled track with the conifer wood on the left and the burn on the right.

> ### WHILE YOU'RE THERE 🛈
> **Coldstream** is only a few miles away, marking the border with England. The town gave its name to the regiment of Coldstream Guards, the oldest regiment in continuous existence in the British Army. Eloping couples from England used to come here to get married – you were allowed to marry younger in Scotland than in England.

⑤ Follow this track, crossing a cattle grid, then leave St Cuthbert's Way and join the track on the right. Follow this, passing a **sheepfold** then two conifer plantations. The track eventually winds upwards, skirts a hill, then descends to **Trowupburn farmhouse**. Walk in front of the farm buildings then bear right to a fingerpost.

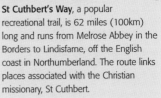

> ### WHAT TO LOOK FOR 🛈
> **St Cuthbert's Way**, a popular recreational trail, is 62 miles (100km) long and runs from Melrose Abbey in the Borders to Lindisfarne, off the English coast in Northumberland. The route links places associated with the Christian missionary, St Cuthbert.

⑥ Go through the gate here and follow the sign 'Border Ridge 1½'. Wander along this wide grassy track then cross the ford next to the very large sheepfold. Maintain direction with the burn now on your right, then cross the burn again, nip over the stile and join the sheep track that bears left through the bracken.

⑦ Walk round the hill and, when you are parallel with the sheepfold on the left, bear right so that the valley of the **Wide Open burn** is on your left, the sheepfold behind you. Work your way uphill through the bracken to the head of the burn until you reach a fence on the higher ground.

⑧ Go through the gate at the corner and maintain direction across open ground – the views are glorious. Walk down to cross a burn and continue ahead, crossing the border into Scotland, then bearing right along the Pennine Way. At the fingerpost follow the track downhill and walk back down across the burn to your starting place.

Stepping Back in Time at Manderston

Quiet lanes take you through gentle countryside and past a fine Edwardian mansion.

•DISTANCE•	4½ miles (7.2km)
•MINIMUM TIME•	2hrs 30min
•ASCENT / GRADIENT•	230ft (70m) ▲ ▲ ▲
•LEVEL OF DIFFICULTY•	🚶 🚶 🚶
•PATHS•	Quiet roads and firm tracks
•LANDSCAPE•	Fields, pasture and mixed woodland
•SUGGESTED MAP•	aqua3 OS Explorer 346 Berwick-upon-Tweed
•START / FINISH•	Grid reference: NT 785539
•DOG FRIENDLINESS•	Good, can run free for much of walk
•PARKING•	Long-stay car park near Duns Market Square
•PUBLIC TOILETS•	Duns

BACKGROUND TO THE WALK

> '*It is not expected that you take the trouble to remember the names of all your Staff. Indeed, in order to avoid obliging you to converse with them, Lower Servants will endeavour to make themselves invisible to you. As such they should not be acknowledged*'
>
> from *How to Address your Servants*
> The Edwardian Country House

Ah, the good old days, when the lower orders knew their place. Such strict social divisions and rigid etiquette sound as if they belong to the ancient past, and seem risible today – yet rules like this were still being observed in grand houses in Britain in the early part of the 20th century. In fact the Edwardian era was a time when the class hierarchy was perhaps more rigid than at any other time.

Biscuit Barons

Rules would certainly have been strictly observed at Manderston, the elegant mansion that you pass on this walk. The home of Lord and Lady Palmer (of Huntley and Palmers biscuit fame), the house you see today was commissioned by Sir James Miller – a wealthy baronet who had married into the aristocracy and wanted to show off his wealth and newly elevated status. No expense was spared and the interior, completed in 1905, is a superb example of Edwardian design – the unique silver staircase is particularly stunning. The family lived in luxury, served by a vast army of servants who catered to their every need. It was the obvious choice of location for Channel 4's reality TV series, *The Edwardian Country House* (2002), when a group of people volunteered to live as Edwardians for three months – some as masters and others as servants. The series revealed just how disciplined life was at Manderston – and how the servants had just as strict a social hierarchy as the upper classes.

The scullery maid, the lowest of the low, was expected to get up at 6AM, light the kitchen range, make tea and empty the chamber pots belonging to the other female servants. She would have to eat her meals in the kitchen, rather than in the Servants' Hall with the others, and would only be allowed above stairs once a day to attend prayer. In comparison, the butler was the head of the household staff and would have been treated with great respect.

Manderston's heyday was shortlived, brought to an end by the outbreak of the First World War, which saw both masters and their servants suffering on the front line in France and Flanders. Social divisions were changed for ever and the army of servants never returned to the house. You can visit Manderston and see the servants' quarters, as well as the opulent rooms upstairs. But remember, you must make way if you meet one of your betters on the stairs…

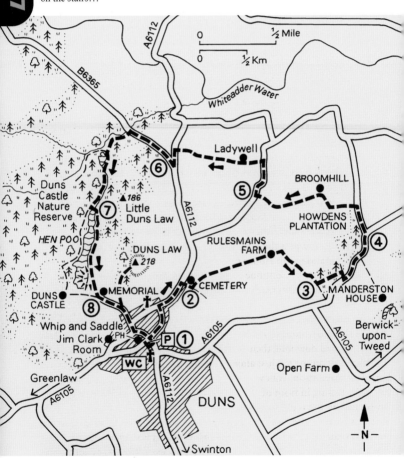

Walk 17 **Directions**

① From the **Market Square** walk north east, turn left along **Currie Street** then right up **Easter Street**. At the main road, turn right and walk to the edge of the town. When you reach a cemetery, turn right and follow the metalled track. Where it splits, bear left.

② With agricultural land on either side, follow the track to reach

Rulesmains Farm. Walk through the farmyard, maintaining direction to reach a gate. Turn sharp right in front of the gate and follow the wide, grassy track. Follow the path as it takes you down to a wood. After about 100yds (91m), take the track on your left that runs through the trees.

③ Follow this path through the woods until you come to a crossing of paths, then turn right. After a few paces you reach a road. Turn left and follow the road as it takes you past a deep grassy valley. After a short distance, you pass the entrance to **Manderston House** on your right-hand side. Continue walking ahead until you reach a fork in the road.

④ Take the left-hand fork and follow the road downhill, then take the track on the left just after **Howdens Plantation**. Follow the path, passing in front of **Broomhill** on the right. Continue ahead to cross a cattle grid and join another road.

⑤ Turn right and follow the road, then take the track on the left that runs between some cottages. Follow the track between fields and under a line of pylons. When you reach the main road turn left, then take the turning to the right signposted to Abbey St Bathans, Cranshaw and Gifford.

⑥ Follow the road, then take the turning on the left-hand side that leads into the wildlife reserve. Follow the track signposted 'Hen Poo', which is the name of a lake. You pass a pond on your right and will then come to the head of **Hen Poo**. Turn left here.

⑦ Keeping the lake on your right, follow the track as it bears to the right, around the water. Continue, to go over a cattle grid and, after a short distance, you will be rewarded with a great view of Duns Castle. Walk to reach the castle entrance on your right.

⑧ Turn left, walk past the **memorial** to John Duns Scotus and continue. When you reach a signpost on your left, you can follow this to climb **Duns Law**. Otherwise just follow the road, go through the arch, walk down **Castle Street** and continue ahead to reach the start of the walk in the **Market Square** in Duns.

Walk 18

A Windy Walk to St Abb's Head

A refreshing wildlife walk along the cliffs.

•DISTANCE•	4 miles (6.4km)
•MINIMUM TIME•	1hr 30min
•ASCENT / GRADIENT•	443ft (135m) ▲▲▲
•LEVEL OF DIFFICULTY•	林林 林林 林林
•PATHS•	Clear footpaths and established tracks
•LANDSCAPE•	Dramatic cliff tops and lonely lighthouse
•SUGGESTED MAP•	aqua3 OS Explorer 346 Berwick-upon-Tweed
•START / FINISH•	Grid reference: NT 913674
•DOG FRIENDLINESS•	They'll love the fresh air, but keep on lead by cliffs
•PARKING•	At visitor centre
•PUBLIC TOILETS•	At visitor centre

BACKGROUND TO THE WALK

St Abb's Head is one of those places that people forget to visit. You only ever seem to hear it mentioned on the shipping forecast – and its name is generally followed by a rather chilly outlook – along the lines of 'north easterly five, continuous light drizzle, poor'. In fact you could be forgiven for wondering if it even exists or is simply a mysterious expanse of sea – like Dogger, Fisher or German Bight.

But St Abb's Head does exist, as you'll find out on this lovely windswept walk which will rumple your hair and leave the salty tang of the sea lingering on your lips. The dramatic cliffs, along which you walk to reach the lonely lighthouse, form an ideal home for thousands of nesting seabirds as they provide superb protection from mammalian predators. Birds you might spot on this walk include guillemots, razorbills, kittiwakes, herring gulls, shags and fulmars – as well as a few puffins.

Guillemots and razorbills are difficult to differentiate, as they're both black and white, and have an upright stance – rather like small, perky penguins. However, you should be able to spot the difference if you've got binoculars as razorbills have distinctive blunt beaks. Both birds belong to the auk family, the most famous member of which is probably the great auk, which went the way of the dodo and became extinct in 1844 – a victim of the contemporary passion for egg collecting.

Luckily no egg collector could scale these cliffs, which are precipitous and surrounded by treacherous seas. Do this walk in the nesting season (May to July) and you may well see young birds jumping off the high cliff ledge into the open sea below. Even though they can't yet fly, as their wings are little more than stubs, the baby birds are nevertheless excellent swimmers and have a better chance of survival in the water than in their nests – where they could fall prey to marauding gulls. Neither razorbills nor guillemots are particularly agile in the air, but they swim with the ease of seals, using their wings and feet to propel and steer their sleek little bodies as they fish beneath the waves.

While the steep cliffs are home to most of the seabirds round St Abb's Head, the low, flat rocks below are also used by wildlife, as they are the favoured nesting site of shags. These large black birds are almost indistinguishable from cormorants – except for the distinctive crest on their heads that gives them a quizzical appearance. They tend to fly low over the water – in contrast to the graceful fulmars that frequently soar along the cliff tops as you walk, hitching a ride on convenient currents of air.

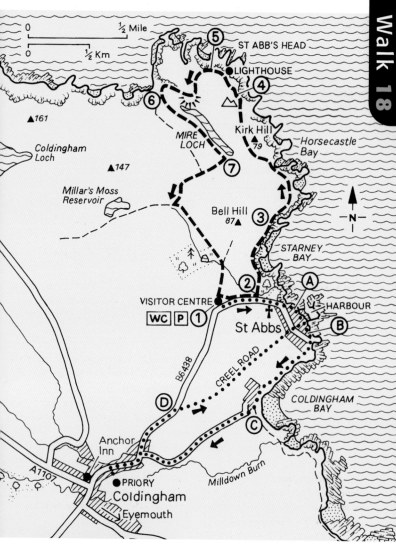

Walk 18 Directions

① From the car park, take the path that runs past the information board and the play area. Walk past the **visitor centre**, then take the footpath on the left, parallel to the main road. At the end of the path turn left and go through a kissing gate – you'll immediately get great views of the sea.

② Follow the track, pass the sign to Starney Bay and continue, passing fields on your left-hand side. Your

> ### *WHERE TO EAT AND DRINK* ⓘ
> The **St Abb's Head Coffee Shop** at the visitor centre is open from Easter to October and serves a great range of sandwiches and light meals. You can choose from things like crab sandwiches, courgette and broccoli soup, toasted sandwiches, huge toasted teacakes and freshly baked cakes and scones. In Coldingham, the **Anchor Inn** serves a good selection of bar meals.

track now winds around the edge of the bay – to your right is the little harbour at St Abbs. The track then winds around the cliff edge, past dramatic rock formations and eventually to some steps.

③ Walk down the steps, then follow the grassy track as it bears left, with a fence on the left. Go up a slope, over a stile and maintain direction on the obvious grassy track. The path soon veers away from the cliff edge, past high ground on the right, then runs up a short, steep slope to a crossing of tracks.

> ### *WHAT TO LOOK FOR* ⓘ
> One of the plants that grows on the cliffs is **scurvy grass**. You can spot it by its heart-shaped leaves and white flowers. It's high in vitamin C and was used by early sailors as a cure for scurvy.

④ Maintain direction by taking the left-hand track which runs up a slope. You'll soon get great views of the **St Abb's Head lighthouse** ahead, dramatically situated on the cliff's edge. Continue to the lighthouse and walk in front of the lighthouse buildings and down to join a tarmac road.

⑤ Follow this road which takes you away from the cliff edge. Continue to an obvious bend, from where you get your first views of the

> ### *WHILE YOU'RE THERE* ⓘ
> Just along the coast from St Abbs is the little village of **Eyemouth** – the haunt of smugglers in the 18th and 19th centuries. It has been a fishing port since the 13th century and the industry still flourishes here today. If you go into the little museum you can see the Eyemouth Tapestry, which was made by local people to mark the centenary of the Great Disaster of 1881, when 189 fishermen died during a terrible storm.

Mire Loch below. You now follow the path downhill to the right, to reach a cattle grid.

⑥ Turn left here to pick up the narrow track by the loch, with the wall on your right-hand side. It's pretty overgrown at the start so can be hard to find, but it soon becomes much more obvious. Walk beside the loch and continue until you reach a gate.

⑦ Turn right along the wide track and walk up to the road. Go left now and continue to cross a cattle grid. When you reach a bend in the road, follow the tarmac track as it bears left. You'll soon go through a gate, then pass some cottages before reaching the car park on the left-hand side.

And on to the Village of Coldingham

A loop to St Abbs harbour and peaceful Coldingham, which is surprisingly rich in history.

See map and information panel for Walk 18

•DISTANCE•	2½ miles (4km)
•MINIMUM TIME•	1hr
•ASCENT / GRADIENT•	197ft (60m) ▲▲▲
•LEVEL OF DIFFICULTY•	👫 👫 👫

Walk 19 Directions (Walk 18 option)

From Point ①, walk past the car park and along the road, following the safe footpaths on either side of the road, to pass the church. You soon reach a small **museum** on the right-hand side. Continue down to reach the pretty little harbour (Point Ⓐ) in the village of **St Abbs**, then work your way back uphill, past some small cottages, to reach **Castle Rock** guest house. Here (Point Ⓑ) follow the coastal footpath, signposted 'to Coldingham Sands'. It's a solid track, dotted with seats so you can sit and enjoy the view. When you reach **Coldingham Bay**, bear right on the track that swings uphill. You will come out at a post-box at **St Vidas Hotel**. Take the footpath (Point Ⓒ) that runs parallel to the road and follow it into **Coldingham**. Turn left here if you want to visit the **priory** in the village, otherwise turn right towards St Abbs. At a lay-by, turn right to join the **Creel Road** (Point Ⓓ) and follow it all the way back to **St Abbs**. This path was used for well over a thousand years by local fishermen and the monks of Coldingham Priory. At the end of the path, turn left and retrace your steps to the car park.

WHILE YOU'RE THERE

Coldingham and St Abbs seem like sleepy little places, yet for centuries they were busy settlements and important religious centres. A Bronze-Age cemetery was discovered near Coldingham village and Roman pottery and glass beads have also been found. In AD 635, an early Christian missionary – possibly St Finnian – came here from Iona. He founded an ecclesiastical centre, either at St Abb's Head or in Coldingham, and was followed by St Ebba, sister of King Oswy of Northumbria (from whom St Abbs takes its name). Some think that she had turned to religious life in order to escape an arranged marriage – whatever the reason for her arrival, she soon established a monastery at Kirk Hill on St Abb's Head. This was destroyed by Vikings in the 9th century – all that remains today are faint outlines of buildings in the turf. Nearby **Coldingham Priory** was founded in 1098 by King Edgar of Scotland for Benedictine monks from Durham. It was frequently damaged in border conflicts with England and almost destroyed by Cromwell in 1648. The priory was rebuilt after the Restoration and still functions as a church today.

Walk 20

Dunbar – John Muir's Home Town

This easy walk takes you to a coastal country park, passing the home of the conservationist John Muir.

•DISTANCE•	5 miles (8km)
•MINIMUM TIME•	1hr 45min
•ASCENT / GRADIENT•	49ft (15m) ▲ ▲ ▲
•LEVEL OF DIFFICULTY•	材 材 材
•PATHS•	Town streets and wide firm tracks, some soft sand
•LANDSCAPE•	Golden sands and rugged rocks
•SUGGESTED MAP•	aqua3 OS Explorer 351 Dunbar & North Berwick
•START / FINISH•	Grid reference: NT 680788
•DOG FRIENDLINESS•	On lead by golf course and in town, can run free on beach
•PARKING•	On High Street in Dunbar
•PUBLIC TOILETS•	By leisure centre in Dunbar

Walk 20 Directions

This walk takes you through the little town of Dunbar and along the coast to John Muir Country Park, a large area that encompasses many different habitats. Dunbar was a traditional Scottish seaside resort and still retains a bucket and spade appeal, making it popular with families.

From the **post office** in Dunbar, turn right down the **High Street**. You'll soon pass an attractive statue of a young John Muir, which stands outside the town museum. John Muir was born in the town in 1838 and lived here until his family emigrated to America, settling in Wisconsin. Muir had always loved wildlife and after he nearly lost his sight in an industrial accident (up to then he had been an ingenious inventor), he resolved to dedicate his life to protecting nature. He travelled widely and explored much

of the American west, particularly around Yosemite. He became a farmer and was a pioneering conservationist, campaigning vigorously for a national park in America. His ideas were eventually approved and Yosemite National Park was created. Muir continued to promote the idea of conservation and wrote a number of books including *Our National Parks* (1901) and *The Yosemite* (1912).

Further down the street you pass **John Muir House**, on the left-hand side of the road. This was Muir's childhood home. A bit further down the street is the tourist

---

WHAT TO LOOK FOR ⓘ

Dunbar Town House Museum is one of the oldest buildings in the town. It was once a prison and has displays on the dark side of Dunbar's history, as well as an exhibition that demonstrates just how much the lives of children in the town have changed over the past hundred years.

information centre. When you reach the bottom of the street bear left and walk past the **leisure centre**. Continue along the road then take the path on the right, signed 'Clifftop Trail'. The beach soon comes into view and you come to a crossing of tracks where you take the steps that lead under a small arch. John Muir had fond memories of the coastline here – and of some very dramatic storms. He once wrote: 'I loved to wander… along the sea-shore to gaze at the shells and seaweeds… and best of all to watch the waves in awful storms thundering on the black headlands and craggy ruins of the old Dunbar Castle…' (*The Story of My Boyhood and Youth*, 1913).

> ### WHERE TO EAT AND DRINK ⓘ
> In Dunbar itself there are several pubs and an Italian restaurant, but one of the most popular places in town is the **Ocean Fish Bar** on the High Street by the tourist information centre. You can get crispy fish and chips or tasty pizzas and eat them down by the sea. If you really want a treat, drive further along the coast to **Greywalls**, a swish hotel with a garden designed by Gertrude Jekyll. They do good tea and shortbread.

> ### WHILE YOU'RE THERE ⓘ
> The **Scottish Seabird Centre** in North Berwick is a great place to take children. It's a bit like a hi-tech bird hide, as there are screens displaying live pictures of the gannet colony that lives on the Bass Rock out in the Firth of Forth. You can control the cameras yourself from the centre, zooming in and panning as you choose. In spring you can also watch puffins and in winter the cameras are focused on a nearby seal colony.

You're now on a wide firm track, with the sea to your right. As you walk you'll pass a **war memorial** and then some striking rock formations. Your path soon brings you up to a viewpoint and information board giving you some details on the wildlife of the area. Some of the plants you might spot are birdsfoot trefoil, stonecrop and common wild thyme.

Continue now to go down a flight of steps on the left-hand side which takes you on to a golf course. Walk round the edge of the course, past the clubhouse on the left-hand side and round the shore. When you reach the holiday chalets, go past them and then walk to your left. There's a lovely sandy beach on your right-hand side, with a bridge on the sands.

Continue walking, then turn right to follow the track that runs past a large pool. At the end turn left, then go over the wooden footbridge on the right. Once you're over the bridge turn right and then left, following the track that hugs the wall. The sands of **Belhaven Bay** are now on your right. Your way now takes you into the woods or you can follow the shoreline along the dunes – as you prefer. In the summer you might spot skylarks or lapwings in the dunes. During the winter keep an eye out for birds such as wigeon, bar-tailed godwit and whooper swan.

Walk to the end of the wood, then retrace your steps to cross the small footbridge again. Turn left, walk back along the track by the pool and then turn left. After a few paces, turn right to walk along **Back Road**, a long straight residential street. At the end of the street turn right, walk past the leisure centre again and back along the **High Street** to your starting place.

Walk 21

Soldiers and Saints on the Pentlands

A lovely, bracing walk across the hills and past Edinburgh's reservoirs.

•DISTANCE•	7 miles (11.3km)
•MINIMUM TIME•	3hrs
•ASCENT / GRADIENT•	837ft (255m) ▲▲▲
•LEVEL OF DIFFICULTY•	林 林 林
•PATHS•	Wide firm tracks, short stretches can be muddy, 3 stiles
•LANDSCAPE•	Reservoirs, fields and hills
•SUGGESTED MAP•	aqua3 OS Explorer 344 Pentland Hills
•START / FINISH•	Grid reference: NT 212679
•DOG FRIENDLINESS•	Good, can run free for much of route
•PARKING•	Car park at end of Bonaly Road, by Edinburgh bypass
•PUBLIC TOILETS•	None on route

BACKGROUND TO THE WALK

Although this walk starts from Edinburgh's busy city bypass, you'll soon think that you're miles from the city. The Pentlands are an uncompromising range of hills, which clasp the city in their craggy, green arms. Their peaks rise 1,500ft (457m) above the sea and offer many great walks where you can easily escape the crowds.

This walk takes you past several reservoirs, which keep Scotland's capital supplied with water. The first you pass is Torduff Reservoir, which was built in 1851 and is 72ft (22m) deep. Later on you come down to Glencorse Reservoir. Beneath its waters are concealed the remains of the Chapel of St Katherine's (or Catherine's) in the Hopes. This dates back to the 13th century and the reign of Robert the Bruce. If it's been extremely dry (unlikely, I know) and the waters are shallow, you might even see it peering out above the surface.

By coincidence (or perhaps not), in Mortonhall, on the other side of the bypass, is the site of St Catherine's Balm Well, or Oily Well. Tradition has it that St Catherine travelled through here carrying holy oil from Mount Sinai. She dropped a little and the well appeared in answer to her prayers. The oily water was said to heal skin diseases and attracted many pilgrims. The nearby suburb of Liberton is a corruption of 'leper town'. A modern explanation for the oily water was deposits of paraffin shale. James VI visited the spot in 1617 and ordered that the well be protected by a building. This was destroyed by Cromwell's troops when they camped on the surrounding hills in 1650. Cromwell, who had been helped to victory in England by the Scottish Covenanters, had fallen out with them after they decided to recognise Charles II as King.

The Pentlands are full of similar military memories. The Camus Stone near Farmilehead commemorates a battle fought against the Danes. A large number of human remains were found beneath it. And in 1666, General Dalyell of The Binns (an ancestor of MP Tam Dalyell) beat a Covenanting force at Rullion Green on these hills, crushing the so-called Pentland Rising. These days you may still see soldiers on the Pentlands, for there are army firing ranges at Castlelaw, while recruits from training barracks at nearby Glencorse and Redford are often put through their paces on the hills.

Lord Cockburn's Inspiration

In the final stages of this bracing walk you'll pass Bonaly Tower, once the home of Lord Cockburn (1779–1854), writer and judge, who was inspired by his glorious surroundings to pen the words: 'Pentlands high hills raise their heather-crowned crest, Peerless Edina expands her white breast, Beauty and grandeur are blent in the scene, Bonnie Bonally lies smiling between.'

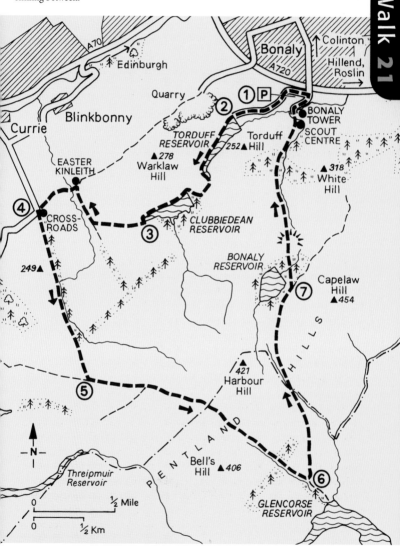

Walk 21 Directions

① From the car park by the bypass, follow the signs pointing in the direction of Easter Kinleith and walk along the metalled track. You will reach the **water treatment works** on your left-hand side. Continue on past the works to reach the gate by the East of Scotland Water sign.

Walk 21

② Go through the kissing gate and continue walking ahead, keeping **Torduff Reservoir** on your left-hand side. When you reach the top of the reservoir, walk over the little bridge and follow the metalled track as it bends round to the right. Walk under a line of electricity pylons, and go over a small bridge, passing an artificial waterfall on your left-hand side, and continue past **Clubbiedean Reservoir**.

WHAT TO LOOK FOR ⓘ

Colinton, close to the start of this walk, has strong associations with Robert Louis Stevenson whose grandfather, Dr Lewis Balfour, was minister at the local church. Stevenson spent many of his holidays here as a child, exploring the hills and nearby Colinton Dell, an extremely picturesque spot.

③ Your path now bears right, with fields on either side. Pass under another line of pylons and walk to **Easter Kinleith farm**. Now follow the path as it bends back to the left, signposted 'Harlaw'. Pass a sign for Poets' Glen and continue ahead, over a bridge and on to a large white house on the left-hand side called **Crossroads**.

④ Turn left and follow the sign for Glencorse Reservoir. Follow this track, past a conifer plantation on your left-hand side, then cross a stile next to a metal gate. Continue ahead until you reach two more

WHERE TO EAT AND DRINK ⓘ

The **Spylaw Tavern** in Colinton is worth trying for a light lunch, a cool drink or tea or coffee. They've got a beer garden where you can sit outside if it's sunny but be warned it can get a bit smelly. Further along the bypass is the **Flotterstone Inn**, south of Boghall, which serves good pub lunches.

metal gates, where you cross a stile on the left-hand side signposted to Glencorse.

⑤ Follow the track, with the hills on either side, and cross an old stone stile. Continue in the same direction until you come to a copse of conifers on the right-hand side, with **Glencorse Reservoir** ahead. Turn left here, following the sign to Colinton by Bonaly.

⑥ Walk uphill and maintain direction to go through a gap in a wire fence. The track now narrows and takes you through the hills, until it eventually opens out. Continue in the same direction to reach a fence encircling conifers. Keep the fence on your left and walk down to cross a stile on the left-hand side.

WHILE YOU'RE THERE ⓘ

If you're feeling fit then make for **Hillend Ski Centre** on the Pentlands. This is a dry-ski slope, suitable for ski and snowboarding practice. A chairlift takes you to the top if you don't fancy the climb. You're also very close to wonderful **Rosslyn Chapel** (► Walk 22) , which is well worth the visit and just a short drive along the bypass.

⑦ Walk past **Bonaly Reservoir**, then through a kissing gate and walk downhill, getting good views over Edinburgh as you descend. When you reach a wooden gate, go through and continue ahead, walking downhill, with trees on either side. Go through another kissing gate and follow the tarmac path ahead, passing a **Scout Centre** on the right-hand side followed by **Bonaly Tower**. Turn left at the bridge over the bypass and return to the car park at the start of the walk.

The Romance of Rosslyn Glen

Tree-lined paths take you beside a river to a very special ancient chapel in this glorious glen.

•DISTANCE•	5 miles (8km)
•MINIMUM TIME•	2hrs 30min
•ASCENT / GRADIENT•	279ft (85m)
•LEVEL OF DIFFICULTY•	
•PATHS•	Generally good, but can be muddy and slippery
•LANDSCAPE•	Woodland and fields, short sections of road
•SUGGESTED MAP•	aqua3 OS Explorer 344 Pentland Hills
•START / FINISH•	Grid reference: NT 272627
•DOG FRIENDLINESS•	Can mostly run free, steps and climbs might not suit some
•PARKING•	Roslin Glen Country Park car park
•PUBLIC TOILETS•	None on route; nearest at Rosslyn Chapel Visitor Centre

BACKGROUND TO THE WALK

Despite the splendour of its lush woodland, gurgling waters and delicate wild flowers, the most striking feature of romantic Rosslyn Glen is artificial rather than natural. It's Rosslyn Chapel, the exquisite little church that you meet right at the end of this walk. Founded in 1446 by Sir William St Clair, it took 40 years to build and was originally intended to be a much larger structure. If ever I wished that a building could speak, it's this one. Rosslyn Chapel, you see, is perhaps the most mysterious church in Britain.

Curious Carvings

The interior is full of intricate stone carvings, created by foreign masons commissioned by Sir William, who supervised much of the work himself. The carvings are not just rich in biblical imagery, as you might expect, but also depict masonic and pagan symbols. For instance, there are over one hundred images of the 'green man', the pagan figure that once symbolised great goodness – as well as great evil. There is also a depiction of a *danse macabre*, an allegorical representation of death's supremacy over mankind. There are some surprising images too, notably the New World corn carved into a window arch. Just think about it – this was a century before Columbus discovered America. So how did they know what corn looked like? Well, Sir William's grandfather, Prince Henry of Orkney, is thought to have discovered the New World long before Columbus, sailing from Orkney to Nova Scotia in the 14th century. And there is a Native American tribe, the Micmac, who still pass on the tale that a great lord once sailed from the east and taught them to fish with nets.

Crime of Passion

Perhaps the most stunning carving in the chapel is the Apprentice Pillar, an extraordinarily ornate piece of work. It is said that the pillar was carved by a talented apprentice while his master was away. When the master mason returned he was so jealous of the beauty of the work that he killed the boy.

Rosslyn's greatest mysteries come from its associations with the Knights Templar, the medieval order of warrior monks. They were originally formed to protect pilgrims travelling to the Holy Land – and one of their founders was married to a relative of Sir William. The Templars became immensely wealthy and powerful and were eventually persecuted, being accused of immorality and even pagan idolatry. Many fled to Scotland, with help from the freemasons, taking their treasures with them.

The St Clairs have strong masonic links and Rosslyn Chapel is said to have been built as a memorial to the Templars. Some archaeologists think it hides many of their treasures, such as ancient scrolls from Jerusalem, jewels, perhaps the Holy Grail. Some have even speculated that under the Apprentice Pillar is buried the skull of Christ. This little chapel is full of secrets.

Walk 22 Directions

① From the country park car park, walk north east on to the track until you reach the river. Go up the metal stairs, cross the footbridge, then walk ahead, following the path uphill. In summer, the smell of wild garlic will soon waft over you. At the bottom of a flight of steps, turn right, walk under the old castle arch, down some stone steps, then turn to your left.

WHILE YOU'RE THERE ⓘ

Butterfly and Insect World is not far from here at Lasswade, near Dalkeith. It's a great place to bring kids as the enclosures contain loads of beautiful and exotic butterflies in a tropical setting. There are also some separate cages in which an interesting variety of creepy-crawlies are kept.

② Your path now descends and you keep walking ahead, before climbing more steps. The path then ascends again, until you reach a crossing of paths where you turn right and follow the path that runs steeply downhill. Keep going down until you reach the water's edge.

③ Walk to your left, then follow the path as it climbs again – there is a handrail to assist you. At a crossing of paths turn right, following the direction of the river. Your way now takes you high above the river, and you continue ahead to cross a stile. After you cross another stile the view opens out to fields on your left, then takes you closer to the river again. Cross a burn and another stile to the point where the river goes back on itself.

WHERE TO EAT AND DRINK ⓘ

There's a little café in the visitor centre at **Rosslyn Chapel** where you can get teas, coffees and cakes. Otherwise there are two reasonable pubs in the centre of the village. The **Original Rosslyn Hotel** is on your right-hand side as you come into the village and serves bar lunches and high teas. Opposite it, also on the right of your route, is the **Roslin Glen Hotel**, which also does light bar meals such as baked potatoes.

④ Cross the broken fence, then keep ahead, passing an old pollarded tree on the left-hand side. Follow the small sign pointing uphill to **Maiden Castle**. At the top turn left (the sign says 'caution, path erosion'). You now get great views over the river valley as you cross the ridge then keep walking to reach a metal gate.

⑤ Turn left and follow the wide path. You eventually walk past buildings of the **Animal Research Centre**, then pass a **memorial** to the Battle of Rosslyn on your right-hand side. Keep walking straight ahead, through the outskirts of **Roslin** and up to the crossroads at the village centre.

WHAT TO LOOK FOR ⓘ

The **memorial** to the Battle of Rosslyn commemorates a battle between Scotland and England. The carnage of the battle gave rise to many local landscape names such as shinbone field, kilburn and stinking rig – a reference presumably to all the dead bodies left in the fields.

⑥ Turn left here and walk ahead. After a short distance you see **Rosslyn Chapel** on the right-hand side. If you don't intend to visit the chapel, take the path that bears downhill to the right, just in front of it. When you reach the cemetery turn left, following the signpost for 'Polton', and walk between the cemeteries to the metal gate for **Rosslyn Castle**. Go down the steps on the right-hand side, over the bridge again and return to the car park at the start.

Edinburgh's Murky Secrets

A stroll through the atmospheric streets of Edinburgh's Old Town.

•DISTANCE•	2 miles (3.2km)
•MINIMUM TIME•	1hr
•ASCENT / GRADIENT•	197ft (60m) ▲▲▲
•LEVEL OF DIFFICULTY•	🏃 🏃 🏃
•PATHS•	City streets, some hill tracks
•LANDSCAPE•	Atmospheric ancient city and brooding castle
•SUGGESTED MAP•	AA Street by Street Edinburgh
•START / FINISH•	Grid reference: NT 256739
•DOG FRIENDLINESS•	Keep on lead, watch paws don't get trodden on by crowds
•PARKING•	Several NCP car parks in Edinburgh
•PUBLIC TOILETS•	At Waverley Station

BACKGROUND TO THE WALK

Edinburgh is often thought of as an extremely respectable, rather genteel city. But as you'll find out in this walk through the city's ancient heart – the medieval Old Town – it has a darker, more mysterious side to its nature.

The Old Town was the original city and was enclosed by city walls, which protected it from the ravages of conflict – but also stopped it from expanding. This meant that as the population grew, the city became increasingly overcrowded – and was at one time the most densely populated city in Europe. The only solution was to build upwards. People lived in towering tenements known as 'lands', with the wealthy taking the rooms at the bottom, the poorer classes living at the top. Its main street, the Royal Mile, became a complicated maze of narrow 'wynds' or alleyways, which gradually deteriorated into a slum. Cleanliness wasn't a priority and residents habitually threw their rubbish into the street – as well as the contents of their chamber pots. When Dr Johnson stayed in the city with his friend James Boswell, he wrote that they had been 'assailed by the evening effluvia' while walking home from a tavern one night.

A Subterranean Slum

Eventually the tenements became so overcrowded that the decision was made to burrow into the soft sandstone beneath the Royal Mile and create a new network of underground streets and dwellings. It was a subterranean slum. People lived here until the 19th century, when social reforms finally improved conditions in the Old Town and many of the tunnels were sealed. Gradually the secret city disappeared from memory. It wasn't until late in the 20th century that one of these old habitations was opened to the public. Called Mary King's Close, it is full of atmosphere and, as you might expect, is said to be haunted.

Murder in the Dark

There are more dark secrets in the Grassmarket, where the body-snatchers Burke and Hare used to lure their victims before murdering them. They then sold the bodies to a local surgeon who used them in his research. Then there was Deacon Brodie, the seemingly respectable town councillor who had a secret nocturnal life as a criminal and gambler – and was eventually hanged. He was the inspiration for Robert Louis Stevenson's Dr Jekyll – who turned into Mr Hyde, the vicious werewolf, at night. With a history and atmosphere like this, it is hardly surprising that crime writer Ian Rankin sets his Inspector Rebus novels in Edinburgh. He often uses gory historical events in his tales, and has plenty to choose from – even an act of cannibalism which took place in the old Scottish Parliament (*Set in Darkness*, 2000). As Rankin says of Edinburgh – 'It's a very secretive place.'

Walk 23 Directions

① From the main entrance to **Waverley Station**, turn left, go to the end of the street, then cross over

and walk up **Cockburn Street** to the **Royal Mile**, where you turn left and walk downhill. Continue to the black gates of **Holyroodhouse**. Turn right and walk to face the new Parliament visitor centre.

② Turn left and follow the road to the right, then turn right again past **Dynamic Earth** (the building looks like a huge white woodlouse) and walk up into **Holyrood Road**. Turn left, walk past the new buildings of *The Scotsman*, and walk up to **St Mary's Street**, where you turn right and rejoin the **Royal Mile**. Were you to continue ahead you would join the Cowgate, some parts of which were devastated by fire in December 2002.

WHILE YOU'RE THERE ⓘ

Edinburgh Castle dominates the city. Built on an volcano plug, it dates back to the 12th century, although there was a hill fort there long before that. You can see the Honours of Scotland here, the name given to the Scottish Crown Jewels, as well as the Stone of Destiny. The castle was the birthplace of Mary, Queen of Scots' son James – who became James VI of Scotland and later James I of England.

---

③ Turn left, stroll to the main road, then turn left along **South Bridge**. When you reach **Chambers Street** turn right and walk past the museums. At the end of the road, cross and turn left to see the little statue of Greyfriars Bobby, the dog that refused to leave this spot after his master died.

WHERE TO EAT AND DRINK ⓘ

You're spoilt for choice in the city. There are lots of atmospheric pubs dotted around the Old Town so you certainly won't get thirsty. If you prefer tea and cake then try **Plaisir du Chocolat** (they've got umpteen types of hot chocolate and gorgeous cakes) or **Clarinda's**, an excellent traditional tea shop – both at the Holyrood end of the Royal Mile. Also good is **Elephant House**, a relaxed, studenty café on George IV Bridge.

---

④ You can now cross the road and make the short detour into **Greyfriars Kirk** to see where Greyfriars Bobby is buried close to his master. Or simply turn right and walk down **Candlemaker Row**. At the bottom, turn left and wander into the atmospheric **Grassmarket** – once the haunt of Burke and Hare, it's now filled with shops and lively restaurants.

⑤ When you've explored the Grassmarket, walk up winding **Victoria Street** (it says West Bow at the bottom). About two thirds of the way up look out for a flight of steps hidden away on the left. Climb them and when you emerge at the top, walk ahead at the top to join the **Royal Mile** again.

WHAT TO LOOK FOR ⓘ

It's well worth stopping to explore **St Giles' Cathedral**, the main cathedral in Scotland. It was here that John Knox launched the Reformation in Scotland. Look out for the plaque to Jenny Geddes, who threw a stool at the minister during a service. She was furious because he had tried to introduce the English prayer book into Scottish services.

---

⑥ Turn left to walk up and visit the **castle**. Then walk down the **Royal Mile** again, taking a peek into the dark wynds (alleyways) that lead off it. You eventually pass **St Giles' Cathedral** on your right, which is well worth a visit.

⑦ Next on your left you pass the **City Chambers** (under which lie mysterious Mary King's Close). Continue until you reach the junction with **Cockburn Street**. Turn left and walk back down this winding street. At the bottom, cross the road and return to the entrance to **Waverley Station**.

A Climb to Arthur's Seat

A steep climb gives you great views over Edinburgh.
See map and information panel for Walk 23

•DISTANCE•	5 miles (8km)
•MINIMUM TIME•	2hrs
•ASCENT / GRADIENT•	823ft (251m) ▲▲▲
•LEVEL OF DIFFICULTY•	🚶 🚶 🚶

Walk 24 Directions (Walk 23 option)

This walk starts by the Scottish Parliament visitor centre. The Scottish Parliament was established in 1999, following years of vigorous campaigning by those who wanted some form of self-government. The parliament can pass legislation and also alter the rate of tax. Scotland's former parliament was dissolved when Scotland and England were united in 1707. It had been a rather different institution to the English parliament and for centuries had done little more than rubber-stamp the monarch's decisions. It did not even have an established home until the end of the 16th century. Many in the parliament supported the loss of Scottish independence, although others saw it as a national tragedy. After union with England, Scotland retained its separate legal and education systems.

From Point ② on the main walk, turn left and walk round the side of **Holyroodhouse**. The Palace of Holyroodhouse is the Queen's official residence while she is in Scotland and was often used by Queen Victoria on her way to Balmoral. It isn't an opulent residence like Buckingham Palace, but has certainly played its part in history. Bonnie Prince Charlie held court in the Great Gallery here during the Jacobite rebellion in 1745, and it has strong associations with Mary, Queen of Scots. Her secretary David Rizzio was murdered in front of her in the Royal Apartments – an act believed to have been organised by her husband, Lord Darnley.

At the road turn left and follow it round until you come to **St Margaret's Loch** (Point Ⓐ). Make your way around the loch and up the track to reach the ruins of **St Anthony's Chapel**. Follow the path as it takes you past the summit on the right-hand side and continue to join a path that comes up from the left. You now follow the craggy path to the top of **Arthur's Seat** (Point Ⓑ). This excellent viewpoint, named after Arthur, Prince of Strathclyde, is the solidified core of an extinct volcano rising 823ft (251m) above the city. Return to the junction and take the path that's now on the right. Follow it down to **Dunsapie Loch** and join the main track (Point Ⓒ). Turn right and follow the track all the way round. Eventually it brings you back to Point ②, where you turn left and continue on Walk 23.

Walk 25

Go Forth to the Firth

An easy stroll in the shadow of the Forth Bridge.

•DISTANCE•	5 miles (8km)
•MINIMUM TIME•	1hr 45min
•ASCENT / GRADIENT•	197ft (60m) ▲ ▲ ▲
•LEVEL OF DIFFICULTY•	🚶 🚶 🚶
•PATHS•	Firm coastal tracks and quiet roads
•LANDSCAPE•	Secluded estuary and historic bridge
•SUGGESTED MAP•	aqua3 OS Explorer 350 Edinburgh
•START / FINISH•	Grid reference: NT 137784
•DOG FRIENDLINESS•	Signs indicate dogs not allowed on this walk
•PARKING•	On street in South Queensferry
•PUBLIC TOILETS•	South Queensferry

Walk 25 Directions

With your back to the **Hawes Inn**, cross the road to the **Lifeboat Station** and turn right. Take the tarmac path that runs off to the left, underneath the **Forth Bridge**. You'll soon get a good view of Inch Garvie Island. This was used as an ammunition dump during the war and was designed to look like a battleship from the air so as to protect the bridge from bombers. The rocks on the left are often dotted with seals, basking in the sun. Keep following the tarmac track and you'll soon get great views of the bridge behind you. Completed in 1890, it took seven years to build and 57 workers died in its making. A mile and a half

(2.4km) long and 360ft (110m) high, the bridge was a triumph of Victorian engineering and is considered the 19th-century equivalent of the moon landings. It certainly never swayed alarmingly like the new Millennium bridge did over the Thames. It was built just a few years after the Tay Bridge disaster. This bridge linked Fife to Dundee and was blown down during a storm, taking with it a train that was crossing at the time and killing 75 people. The tragedy occurred because the builder, Sir Thomas Bouch, had not made allowances for the fierce Scottish winds. Bouch was due to build the Forth Bridge too, but luckily was replaced by Benjamin Baker, the man who created much of the London Underground. Maintaining the bridge against the elements has always been a battle – so much so that painting the Forth Bridge is now synonymous with a task that never ends.

When you reach **Long Craig Pier** go through a white gate, where there are signs telling you whether the ferry to Cramond is running or not. If it is operational you can walk right along the coast, then use the ferry to cross to Cramond where there's a pleasant pub. The village featured in Muriel Spark's novel *The Prime of Miss Jean Brodie* (1961).

> ### WHILE YOU'RE THERE ⓘ
> **Hopetoun House** near South Queensferry, an elegant Adam mansion, is the ancestral home of the Earls of Hopetoun – now the Marquesses of Linlithgow. There are many art treasures in the house, while the grounds include a deer park and are well worth exploring.

Keep on the track, passing two cottages. Eventually the landscape opens out and you'll see the large tanker berth out in the Forth. Oil is unloaded here, then pumped to a storage depot near Dalmeny. Your track then runs straight ahead until bearing sharp right at **Hound Point**. There is a beautiful stretch of sand here and you get a good view of the islands in the Forth. In front of you is Inchcolm Island; to the right is Oxcars, which has a lighthouse on its crags; then there are two rocks known as Cow and Calves and over to the right is Inchmickery island. Behind them you see the Isle of May, a National Nature Reserve and home to a large population of seabirds. It contains the remains of a Benedictine priory and is topped with a lighthouse built by Robert Louis Stevenson's grandfather.

Your way then takes you past **Fishery Cottage** on the left-hand side, then through another white gate. At a branching of tracks, maintain direction along the coast to follow the **Cramond Walk**. Eventually you'll pass the gate to

Barnbougle Castle on the left-hand side and your path then leads up to get great views of Dalmeny House, the palatial home of the Earls of Rosebery. It has a large collection of French furniture, tapestries and paintings by Gainsborough, Raeburn and Reynolds. Walk around the house, then bear right to walk past the green statue of the horse. Follow the long straight road until you reach the gates at the entrance to the house. Cross the main road with care and continue walking along the road in front of you. This will eventually bring you into **Dalmeny** village, which has a lovely little Norman church.

Turn right at the war memorial and walk downhill – you'll see the bridge again. Turn left along **Station Road**, walk under the railway bridge then turn right immediately to follow the narrow path by the new housing estate. Go up some steps at the end to cross a bridge over an old railway line. Then turn left and walk round the margin of the fenced area (used by the company working on the bridge). When you reach the other side you'll see a long flight of steps running down to the left. Walk down these to come out at the bridge again. Turn left and walk back to the **Hawes Inn**, where Robert Louis Stevenson stayed while he wrote *Kidnapped*.

> ### WHAT TO LOOK FOR ⓘ
> **Inchcolm Island** in the Forth is the site of a beautiful ruined abbey, founded in 1124 by Alexander I. It's also home to many seabirds and a large seal colony. You can take a boat trip out to the island on the *Maid of the Forth*, which sails from the Hawes Pier from Easter to October. If you're lucky you might even spot dolphins and porpoises en route.

Edinburgh's Elegant New Town

A walk in the footsteps of literary giants.

•DISTANCE•	3 miles (4.8km)
•MINIMUM TIME•	1hr 30min
•ASCENT / GRADIENT•	164ft (50m) ▲▲ ▲▲
•LEVEL OF DIFFICULTY•	🚶 🚶 🚶
•PATHS•	Busy city streets
•LANDSCAPE•	Elegant Georgian townscape
•SUGGESTED MAP•	AA Street by Street Edinburgh
•START / FINISH•	Grid reference: NT 257739
•DOG FRIENDLINESS•	Keep on lead, not allowed in Botanic Gardens
•PARKING•	Several large car parks in central Edinburgh
•PUBLIC TOILETS•	At Waverley Station

BACKGROUND TO THE WALK

Don't worry, I'm not going to take you through some dreary 20th-century housing scheme. Edinburgh's New Town was built in the 18th century and is an elegant development of wide airy streets, punctuated with sweeping crescents and lined with soft grey Georgian buildings. It was a planned development, designed to move the focus of the city away from the filthy, overcrowded streets of the medieval Old Town. It was laid out in the mid-18th century by James Craig, a young architect who won a competition for the design. It is separated from the Old Town by Princes Street, the main thoroughfare and once the smartest shopping street in Scotland. In later years Robert Adam contributed to the development, notably designing Charlotte Square in 1791.

Luring the Literati

Houses in the New Town were soon the most coveted in the city and became the haunt of the Scottish literati. Literary associations abound. Kenneth Grahame, author of *The Wind in the Willows* (1908) was born at 30 Castle Street in 1859; Robert Louis Stevenson grew up at 17 Heriot Row; Percy Bysshe Shelley stayed at 60 George Street with his runaway teenage bride in 1811, and Sir Walter Scott once lived at 39 Castle Street.

The city seems to hold a fascination for writers and many historic meetings have taken place here – including that between Walter Scott and Robert Burns. The war poet Wilfred Owen often came into Edinburgh while he was recuperating from 'shell shock' at nearby Craiglockhart War Hospital. One of his early poems was entitled *Six O'clock in Princes Street*. It was at Craiglockhart that Owen met Siegfried Sassoon, already an acclaimed poet, who encouraged him in his writing and made amendments to early drafts of some of his greatest works. Owen left Edinburgh in 1917 and returned to the Front, where he died on 4 November 1918.

Another New Town location, Milne's Bar on Hanover Street, was a favourite haunt of several of Scotland's most influential modern poets. Hugh MacDiarmid (▶ Walk 3) and his two friends and drinking partners Norman MacCaig and Sorley MacLean are just some of the figures who used to meet here in the last century, and the pub walls are still covered with their memorabilia.

In the latter stages of this walk you will pass a statue of Sherlock Holmes, a tribute to his Edinburgh-born creator Sir Arthur Conan Doyle, who lived near by at 11 Picardy Place (which has now been demolished). Conan Doyle studied medicine at Edinburgh University and modelled his fictional detective Holmes on one of his former lecturers – Dr Joseph Bell. Bell was an extremely observant individual and combined his instincts with science to help the police in solving several murders in the city. Many believe that Conan Doyle assisted Bell with his work in this capacity – acting as Dr Watson to his Holmes.

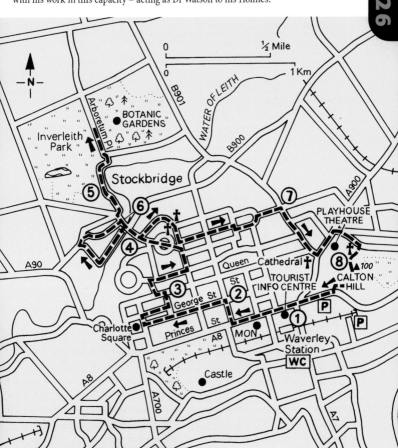

Walk 26 **Directions**

① From the tourist information centre, turn left and walk along **Princes Street**. Just after you pass the **Scott Monument** on your left, cross the road to reach Jenners

department store, Scotland's answer to Harrods. Continue along Princes Street, then take a right turn up **Hanover Street**.

② Take the second turning on your left and walk along **George Street** to **Charlotte Square**. Then turn right and right again to go along **Young Street**. At the end, turn left and walk down **North Castle Street** to reach **Queen Street**.

③ Cross the road, turn left, then right down **Wemyss Place** and right into **Heriot Row**. When you reach **Howe Street** turn left and, before you reach the church in the middle of the street, turn left and walk along **South East Circus Place**. Walk past the sweep of **Royal Circus** and down into **Stockbridge**.

④ Cross the bridge, then turn left along **Dean Terrace**. At the end, turn right into **Ann Street**. When you reach **Dean Park Crescent** turn right and follow the road round into **Leslie Place** and into Stockbridge again. Cross the road to walk down **St Bernard's Row** (it's almost opposite). Follow this, then bear left into **Arboretum Avenue**.

> ### WHILE YOU'RE THERE ℹ
> **Ann Street** in Stockbridge is said to have been the inspiration for J M Barrie's novel *Quality Street* (1901) and was (perhaps still is) one of the most desirable addresses in Scotland. Thomas de Quincey, author of *Confessions of an Opium Eater*, used to visit No 29, the home of Professor John Wilson, who frequently hosted writers and artists here.

⑤ Follow this road as it leads you past the **Water of Leith** and down to **Inverleith Terrace**. Cross over and walk up **Arboretum Place** until you reach the entrance to the **Botanic Gardens** on the right. Turn left after exploring the gardens and retrace your steps to reach **Stockbridge** again.

⑥ Turn left at **Hectors** bar and walk uphill, then turn left along **St Stephen Street**. When you reach

> ### WHERE TO EAT AND DRINK ℹ
> Apart from **Milne's Bar** on Hanover Street there are plenty more pubs and bars to choose from in the New Town. George Street, which is lined with designer stores, has several bistros and restaurants, while down in Stockbridge you can relax in a coffee bar like **Patisserie Florentin**, which serves great cakes, or have a light snack and a cappucino in **Maxi's** or **Hectors**.

the church follow the road, then turn left along **Great King Street**. At the end, turn right, then immediately left to walk along **Drummond Place**, past **Dublin Street** and continue ahead into **London Street**.

⑦ At the roundabout turn right and walk up **Broughton Street** to reach **Picardy Place**. Turn left, walk past the statue of Sherlock Holmes, then bear left towards the **Playhouse Theatre**. Cross over, continue left, then turn right into **Leopold Place** and right again into **Blenheim Place**. At the church turn right, walk up the steps and turn left at the meeting of paths.

⑧ Go up the steps on the right, walk over **Calton Hill**, then turn right to pass the canon. Go downhill, take the steps on your left and walk down into **Regent Road**. Turn right and walk back into **Princes Street** and the start.

> ### WHAT TO LOOK FOR ℹ
> The **Royal Botanic Garden** covers 72 acres (29ha) and contains many plant species that were discovered by early Scottish botanists. Plants were originally grown here in order to research their medicinal qualities. In spring the grounds are full of rhododendrons in bloom, while the glasshouses contain exotic palms, orchids and cacti.

Intoxicating Memories in Leith

A gentle linear walk along the Water of Leith to Edinburgh's ancient port, where claret once flowed in freely.

•DISTANCE•	3½ miles (5.7km)
•MINIMUM TIME•	1hr 30min
•ASCENT / GRADIENT•	Negligible
•LEVEL OF DIFFICULTY•	
•PATHS•	Wide riverside paths and city streets
•LANDSCAPE•	Edinburgh's hidden waterway and revitalised port
•SUGGESTED MAP•	aqua3 OS Explorer 350 Edinburgh
•START•	Grid reference: NT 243739
•FINISH•	Grid reference: NT 271766
•DOG FRIENDLINESS•	Can run free beside water, keep on lead in Leith
•PARKING•	Scottish National Gallery of Modern Art, Belford Road
•PUBLIC TOILETS•	Near Stockbridge

BACKGROUND TO THE WALK

Visitors always forget to come to Leith, yet Edinburgh's ancient seaport is full of history. Even though the docks have been spruced up and become rather trendy, Leith retains an edgy, maritime atmosphere – like an old sea dog who'll spin you a yarn for a pint.

A Taste for Claret

There has been a port at Leith, where the Water of Leith meets the Forth, from at least the 1st century AD when the Romans stored wine for their legions here. The port grew and by medieval times was facilitating valuable trade with France. Ships would leave loaded with dried local fish and return laden with wines, which were landed by the French monks of St Anthony who were based in Edinburgh. One of the main imports was claret, which they sold to wealthy people in the city. It rapidly became Scotland's national drink, whereas the most popular drink in England was port. One old verse sums up its popularity, beginning with the words: 'Guid claret best keeps out the cauld an drives awa the winter soon…' When cargoes arrived, some would be sent on a cart through Leith and anyone who fancied a sample simply turned up with a jug, which would be filled for 6d. It didn't seem to matter how large the jug was.

Whisky Makes its Mark

The quality of the claret imported and bottled in Leith was extremely good. One historian said it 'held in its day a cachet comparable to that which one now associates with Chateau bottled wines.' Claret drinking was seen as a symbol of Scotland's national identity and Jacobites drank it as a symbol of independence.

During the 18th century the British government, determined to price this French drink out of the market, raised taxes on claret. Inevitably traders began to smuggle it into Scotland instead. It was only in the 19th century that claret drinking declined when taxes rose and the Napoleonic Wars made it scarce. While Leith claret was still drunk by the wealthiest people, whisky (a drink from the Highlands) took its place as the people's pick-me-up, going from strength to strength to reach its present state of popularity.

The Darien Expedition

The Port of Leith continued to grow in importance and it was from here, in 1698, that the ill-fated Darien expedition set sail, a venture that was eventually to cost Scotland her independence. The intention was to establish a permanent colony at Darien on the Isthmus of Panama. It cost £400,000 to fund, but it was thought that the venture would give Scotland control of a potentially lucrative trading route. However the terrain was hostile and the colonists rapidly died. The Scottish economy was plunged into crisis and the country was pushed inexorably towards union with England.

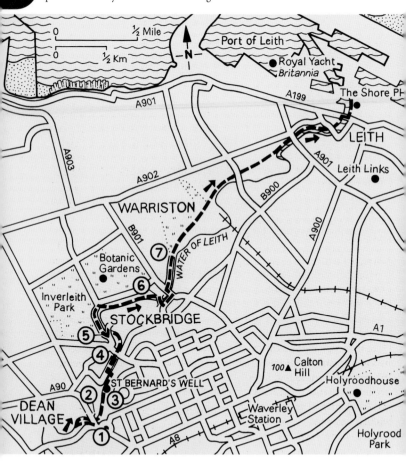

Walk 27 Directions

① From the junction of the **Dean Bridge** and **Queensferry Street**, turn left to walk down **Bell's Brae**.

You are now in the **Dean Village**, which dates back to 1128. It was once a milling centre and had 11 water mills producing all the meal for Edinburgh. At the bottom, turn right into **Miller Row**.

② Follow this to walk under the impressive arches of the **Dean Bridge**, which was designed by Thomas Telford and opened in 1832. Your path then runs along the bottom of the steeply sided gorge, beside the **Water of Leith**, and feels extremely rural. You'll pass an old well on your left, followed by the more impressive **St Bernard's Well**.

③ St Bernard's Well was discovered by some schoolboys in 1760. The mineral water was said to have healing properties and, in 1789, the present Roman Temple was built, with Hygeia – the goddess of health – at the centre. From here continue along the main path, then go up the steps. Turn left, and go right on to **Dean Terrace** to reach **Stockbridge**.

④ Cross the road and go down the steps ahead – immediately to the right of the building with the clock tower. Continue to follow the path

beside the river. Where the path ends, climb on to the road, turn left and then right to go down **Arboretum Avenue**.

⑤ Walk along this road, then turn right along the path marked Rocheid Path. This runs beside the river and is a popular cycleway and jogging path. Follow this, passing the backs of the **Colonies** – low-cost housing built by the Edinburgh Co-operative for artisans in the late 19th century. The idea was to provide houses in a healthy environment away from the dirt of the city. Walk to **Tanfield Bridge**.

⑥ Go right, over the bridge, go up the steps, then turn left, walking towards the clock tower. At the end turn left along **Warriston Place**, cross the road, then turn right down **Warriston Crescent**. This is lined with elegant town houses. Walk to the end where you'll reach the park.

⑦ Bear right, around the edge of the park, then follow the path as it bears uphill between trees. Turn left at the top and follow the cycle track marked 'Leith 1¼'. Follow this all the way into **Leith**, where it brings you out near the old **Custom House**. Bear right then left to walk along **The Shore** and explore the pubs, before returning to town by bus.

Walk 28

Poppy Harvest at East Linton

A delightful and varied walk past an old doo'cot and a picturesque mill to fields where poppies grow.

•DISTANCE•	4½ miles (7.2km)
•MINIMUM TIME•	2hrs 30min
•ASCENT / GRADIENT•	295ft (90m) ▲ ▲ ▲
•LEVEL OF DIFFICULTY•	👫 👫 👫
•PATHS•	Fields paths, river margins and woodland tracks. Short section of busy road, 2 stiles
•LANDSCAPE•	Cultivated fields, lively river and picturesque village
•SUGGESTED MAP•	aqua3 OS Explorer 351 Dunbar & North Berwick
•START / FINISH•	Grid reference: NT 591772
•DOG FRIENDLINESS•	Can run free for many sections – watch for sheep though
•PARKING•	Main street in East Linton
•PUBLIC TOILETS•	None on route; nearest in Haddington

BACKGROUND TO THE WALK

If you were to design your ideal walk, what would it include? A dash of history; a crumbling castle; perhaps some fields of waving corn and a peaceful riverbank? And maybe a pretty village, in which to settle down finally with a cup of tea and a large wedge of home-made cake? Well, this walk's for you then. It takes you on a lovely varied route through the fertile countryside of East Lothian, just a few miles outside Edinburgh. It's the sort of walk that is enjoyable at any time of year – but it is particularly lovely in the summer when you can see all the wild flowers that line your way.

A Phantastic Doo'cot

The first part of the walk takes you past an old doo'cot (dovecote) where pigeons were bred to be used as food. It once belonged to Phantassie house, a local property which was the birthplace of Sir John Rennie in 1761. Rennie was a civil engineer who, after studying at Edinburgh University, moved to London. There he constructed Southwark and Waterloo bridges, as well as designing dockyards, bridges and canals throughout the country.

Not far from the doo'cot is the extremely photogenic Preston Mill, which is owned by the National Trust for Scotland. This is an 18th-century grain mill and was used to process the produce of East Lothian's fertile arable fields. It has a distinctive conical kiln, which was used for drying the grain, and a barn where the grain was ground. The machinery is driven by a waterwheel.

The Symbolism of Poppies

Later on in the walk, as you make your way towards Hailes Castle, you might well see the scarlet heads of poppies waving in among the ripening crops. (I saw them on a hot day in August and they made a magnificent spectacle.) Sadly, this is a sight you see all too rarely these days, as intensive agriculture has virtually eliminated them from the fields, but it would once have been commonplace. Poppies have been a symbol of blood, harvest and regeneration for thousands of years, as they grow in fields of grain and will rapidly colonise disturbed ground – this was most graphically illustrated in the First World War, and poppies have, of course, also become a symbol of remembrance of lives lost.

Poppies were the sacred plant of the Roman crop goddess Ceres (from whose name we get the word 'cereal'). The Romans used to decorate her statues with garlands of poppies and barley, and poppy seeds were offered up during rituals to ensure a good harvest. Poppy seeds mixed with grains of barley have also been found in Egyptian relics dating from 2500 BC. In Britain it was once believed that picking poppies would provoke a storm and they were nicknamed 'thundercup', 'thunderflower' or 'lightnings'. Whatever you call them, they're a glorious and welcome sight.

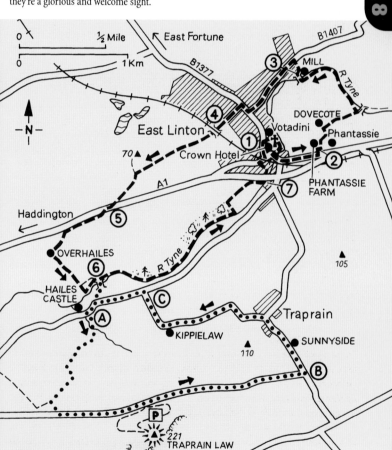

Walk 28 **Directions**

① From the **Market Cross** in the centre of the town, take the path that runs to the left of the church. When you come to the main street

bear left, then walk over the bridge and continue until you reach a garage on the right-hand side. Turn left here into the farm opposite the garage, following the sign for Houston Mill and Mill House.

② Follow the path round the farm buildings until you see the old doo'cot (**dovecote**) ahead of you. Turn right just in front of it and follow the path along the edge of the field. When you reach the footbridge, turn left to continue walking around the edge of the field, with the river on your right-hand side. At the next footbridge, cross over and go through the metal gate.

③ Take the right-hand path across the field and go through the kissing gate to reach the old mill. Once you've inspected the mill – you can go inside when it's open – continue on to meet the main road, then turn left to walk back into the town. Turn right to walk along the **High Street**, then cross over the road and turn left to go down **Langside**.

WHILE YOU'RE THERE

The **Museum of Flight** at East Fortune, near Haddington, is Scotland's national museum of aviation. You can see wartime memorabilia and lots of old aircraft, including a Tigermoth, all housed in old Second World War Nissen huts and hangers. Haddington itself is a prosperous town and was the birthplace of John Knox, the founder of the Presbyterian Church.

---

④ When you reach the recreation ground, maintain direction and walk towards the railway. Go through the underpass and walk ahead through the fields. Continue in the same direction, crossing over three walls with the help of some steps and two stiles. After you cross the third wall the track starts to become indistinct, but maintain direction until you reach a wooden sign. Turn left here to reach the road.

WHERE TO EAT AND DRINK

Votadini is a coffee shop on the main street in East Linton. There are some comfy seats so you can stretch out after your walk, and they serve home-made scones and cakes, as well as light meals such as toasted waffles. For a stronger brew than tea try the **Crown Hotel**, also in the centre of the town.

---

⑤ Turn right, then cross over at the parking place to continue along the track running parallel to the road. Walk to **Overhailes farm**, through the yard, then bear left and follow the wide track down to **Hailes Castle**. Ignore the first path that joins from the left and go a few paces further to turn left along another path that leads to a bridge.

⑥ Don't cross over the bridge but instead follow the track that runs to the left of the steps. You're now walking along the river's edge on a narrow path. Follow the path to cross a stile, walk along a field margin, then enter some woods. Walk up a flight of stairs, then down some steps, and continue following the path to walk under the road bridge.

⑦ The path now runs through a garden and on to the road, where you turn right. Walk under the railway bridge, then turn left and return to the starting point of the walk in the town.

WHAT TO LOOK FOR

Hailes Castle, the ruins of which you'll see down by the Tyne, dates back to the 13th century. It was one of the places where Mary, Queen of Scots (goodness, didn't that woman get around!) stayed when she and Bothwell were fleeing from their enemies. The castle was eventually destroyed by Cromwell in 1650.

And on to Prehistoric Traprain Law

A longer walk to the site of a prehistoric hill fort.
See map and information panel for Walk 28

•DISTANCE•	4 miles (6.4km)
•MINIMUM TIME•	2hrs
•ASCENT / GRADIENT•	246ft (75m) ▲▲▲
•LEVEL OF DIFFICULTY•	🚶🚶 🚶🚶 🚶

Walk 29 Directions (Walk 28 option)

At Point ⑥ on the main route, cross the bridge over the river and walk up the gravel track – it can get overgrown in summer with nettles and brambles. Continue following the path, bearing right along the road. When you reach **Hailes Castle** on the right-hand side, take the turning opposite on the left – Point Ⓐ. Go through the green metal gate and follow the path as it bears right and becomes an enclosed track, with a wall on the left-hand side. Walk until you reach a gate saying 'farm road only', and take the turning on the left. Continue, to go through a gate and join the road, where you turn left. It's a bit of a long tramp now along the road and, though it's not too busy, do keep an eye out for cars. Eventually you'll reach **Traprain Law** on the right-hand side. To enjoy the views, make a detour to climb the law, which you reach via a stile. It was the site of a prehistoric hill fort. In 1919 a deep pit was discovered on the law, filled with an extraordinary collection of 4th-century silver plate, which

had been crushed into pieces as if it was going to be melted down. Some think that it had been hidden there by Angle or Saxon thieves, early in the 5th century AD.

Otherwise continue along the road, pass the car park on the right-hand side and walk to the junction – Point Ⓑ. Turn left here, walk up past **Sunnyside house**, then turn left following the sign to Kippielaw. You now continue on this quiet tarmac road, walk past **Kippielaw house**, then follow the road as it bears right and goes downhill. At the bottom of the hill, Point Ⓒ, turn left and walk back towards **Hailes Castle**. Turn right just in front of the castle, walk back over the footbridge, then turn sharp right, almost doubling back on yourself to walk along the river and rejoin the main route at Point ⑥.

WHILE YOU'RE THERE ⓘ

Lennoxlove House, close to Haddington, is the family seat of the Duke of Hamilton. The house, which dates back to medieval times, is open to the public and contains a number of fine pieces of furniture and paintings. You can also see the death mask of Mary, Queen of Scots and the casket in which she kept her letters.

Walk 30

The Romance of Linlithgow

An easy circuit of Linlithgow Loch and memories of a tragic queen.

•DISTANCE•	3 miles (4.8km)
•MINIMUM TIME•	1hr
•ASCENT / GRADIENT•	Negligible
•LEVEL OF DIFFICULTY•	
•PATHS•	Town streets and firm tracks
•LANDSCAPE•	Romantic loch and bustling town centre
•SUGGESTED MAP•	aqua3 OS Explorer 349 Falkirk, Cumbernauld & Livingston
•START / FINISH•	Grid reference: NT 001771
•DOG FRIENDLINESS•	Loch popular with dog walkers – keep on lead in town
•PARKING•	The Vennel car park by tourist information centre
•PUBLIC TOILETS•	The Vennel off Linlithgow High Street

Walk 30 Directions

This easy walk takes you to a hidden section of the Union Canal, around Linlithgow Loch, and past the romantic ruins of Linlithgow Palace – the birthplace of Mary, Queen of Scots. It's suitable for anyone and is particularly good for children.

From the tourist information centre, turn right to walk along the **High Street**. You'll pass **Annet House** on your left, home of Linlithgow Museum, and should then turn left to walk up **Lion Well Wynd**. When you reach the top, turn right for a few paces and then bear left to cross the railway bridge. Turn left on the other side of the bridge and follow the road. You'll get good views over Linlithgow Palace from here. You'll eventually come to an area of grass on the right-hand side, and a 16th-century dovecote on the left. Bear right here for a few paces, then continue ahead and turn right to cross the bridge over the canal. Turn right

again to visit the **Canal Centre**. There's a little museum here where you can see old photographs and artefacts associated with the Union Canal. You can take boat trips to visit the new Falkirk Wheel (► Walk 31), which links the Union and Forth and Clyde canals.

Walk back over the bridge and turn right, then sharp left. Walk back on yourself for a few paces then turn right, downhill. Follow this road to walk under the railway bridge and past the station, which is on your right-hand side. Continue ahead to reach the **High Street**, then turn left

---

WHAT TO LOOK FOR

You will see plenty of **swans** on the loch. Once eaten at medieval banquets, the swan is now a protected species. However, they still suffer many losses each year, both from overhead power cables, which are a hazard in flight, and from lead poisoning caused when they swallow lead weights discarded by anglers. Swans mate for life and will grieve deeply when a mate dies. They're extremely territorial and will defend their nests and young vigorously.

Walk 30

and walk back to reach the tourist infromation centre on your right-hand side. From the Vennel car park by the town hall, walk down the steps at the far end and down to the loch. Turn right and follow the path – you'll soon see Linlithgow Palace on the right.

WHERE TO EAT AND DRINK

The tea room at the **Canal Centre** does home baking and ice creams and is open daily, 2–5PM, in July and August, and weekends from Easter to October. There's a coffee shop, **The Coffee Neuk**, next to the TIC, and **Caffe La**, next to Annet House, does baguettes, pizzas, salads and sandwiches.

Mary, Queen of Scots was born here in 1542 and inherited the Scottish throne when she was only one week old, after her father James V died a few weeks after facing defeat by the English at the Battle of Solway Moss. Mary is one of the great romantic figures in history and her life was as eventful, and tragic, as an opera. I mean, just listen to this… Sent to France at the age of six to be educated, she was married young to a French prince. Her husband became King, but died soon after. Mary returned to Scotland, fluent in French and Latin – but having probably forgotten her native language. She was married again, this time to Lord Darnley, a vain and weak man. He was manipulated by her enemies into a frenzy of jealousy over her fondness for her secretary David Rizzio – who was murdered before her eyes in Holyroodhouse. Mary realised that she was their real target and escaped, with Darnley, to Dunbar. She later conspired with the Earl of Bothwell to murder her husband. She then married Bothwell, was involved in a battle with her former husband's supporters and was imprisoned on the island of Loch Leven. Later she fled to England, where she was imprisoned by Elizabeth I, who saw her as a threat to the English throne. Eventually Mary was executed at Fotheringhay Castle in 1587, wearing a crimson velvet bodice.

When you reach the children's play area, turn right over the little footbridge that leads away from the loch. Walk up the alleyway, then turn left when you reach the road. Walk until you see **Barons Hill Avenue** on the opposite side. Go through the wooden gate on your left, through a kissing gate and follow the path as it leads back to the loch. Follow the track as it winds round the loch, then go through another kissing gate to reach the road. Turn sharp left and follow the path as it continues round the loch. Continue in the same direction (there are great views of the palace from here) with the loch on your left. Eventually you'll join a tarmac track and come to some houses on the right. Follow the path over another bridge. The path now continues around the loch, then takes you past a parking area on the right and past a fishing lodge. The landing stage is a good place to see the swans that live on the loch. Walk past some modern houses on the right-hand side, and continue following the track until you see the arch. Turn right here and walk back up into the car park.

WHILE YOU'RE THERE

Not far from Linlithgow at Bo'ness is the **Bo'ness and Kinneil Railway**, a privately run steam railway. There's a lovely little restored station and several gleaming, restored locomotives and carriages. They run steam trips throughout the year.

Reinventing the Wheel at Falkirk

A stroll along Scotland's old canal system to see a strikingly modern 21st-century wheel.

•DISTANCE•	2 miles (3.2km); 4 miles (6.4km) with monument
•MINIMUM TIME•	1hr
•ASCENT / GRADIENT•	197ft (60m) ▲ ▲ ▲
•LEVEL OF DIFFICULTY•	旅 旅 旅
•PATHS•	Canal tow paths and town streets
•LANDSCAPE•	Roman wall, 19th-century waterways, 21st-century wheel
•SUGGESTED MAP•	aqua3 OS Explorer 349 Falkirk, Cumbernauld & Livingston
•START / FINISH•	Grid reference: NS 868800
•DOG FRIENDLINESS•	Good along canals – as long as they don't fight other dogs
•PARKING•	Car park at Lock 16, by Union Inn
•PUBLIC TOILETS•	At Falkirk Wheel Visitor Centre

BACKGROUND TO THE WALK

The words 'new' and 'unique' are rather overused these days. They seem to be applied to everything from shades of lipstick to formulations of engine oil. But this walk gives you the chance to see something that fully deserves the epithet. The Falkirk Wheel, which opened in the spring of 2002, is the world's first rotating boat lift. It was designed in order to reconnect the Forth and Clyde and Union canals, which stretch across the central belt of Scotland, and so restore a centuries-old link between Glasgow and Edinburgh.

Cruising the Canals

The Forth and Clyde Canal, which ran from Grangemouth to Glasgow, was completed in 1790 and immediately made a great difference to the Scottish economy. It opened up a lucrative trading route to America – raw materials could now easily be transported east, while finished products could be shipped west. It also meant that coal extracted from the mines in Lanarkshire could be sent into the newly industrialised areas of Glasgow. The canal was so successful that merchants in Edinburgh soon felt that they were missing out on trade. A plan was devised for another waterway, running from Edinburgh to Falkirk. Work on the Union Canal began in 1818 and a flight of locks was constructed to link it to the Forth and Clyde Canal.

Rise and Fall

The canals were used to transport not only goods but also people. Many preferred to travel by barge than by stage coach, as they were far less bumpy and decidedly warmer. Night boats even had dining rooms and gaming tables. By 1835 over 127,000 people were travelling on the canal each year.

However, shortly afterwards the canal craze began to give way to yet another new innovation – the railways. Train travel, which gained in popularity from the middle of the 19th century, offered cheaper and faster transport, leading to the decline of the canal network. They clung to life until the 1960s, when they were broken up by the expanding network of roads. However, the canals have now been recognised as an important part of Scotland's industrial heritage and are being restored. The Falkirk Wheel was built to replace the original flight of locks, which had been removed in the 1930s, and it's as much a work of art as a feat of engineering. The Wheel lifts boats from one canal to another and is the only rotating boat lift in the world. Made of sharply glinting steel, it's 115ft (35m) high and looks rather like a set of spanners that have fallen from a giant's tool kit. It can carry eight boats at a time and lift loads of 600 tonnes – that's roughly equivalent to a hundred elephants, in case you're wondering.

An incongruous sight against the gentle tangle of vegetation beside the canal, the Wheel seems to have re-energised the waterways, waking them from their long slumber and drawing people to it like some monumental magnet.

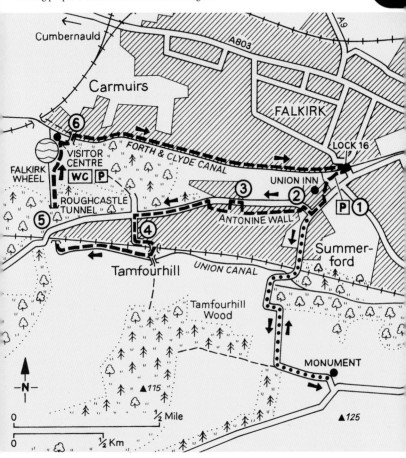

Walk 31 Directions

① Start at the **Union Inn** by Lock 16. This was once one of the best-known pubs in Scotland and

catered for passengers on the canal. Turn right now, away from the canal, then go right along the road. Turn right along **Tamfourhill Road** and go through the kissing gate on the left-hand side of the road.

Alternatively, don't turn up Tamfourhill Road yet, but continue walking uphill to go under the viaduct. Keep walking all the way up until you come to a monument on the left. This commemorates the Battle of Falkirk (1298) in which William Wallace was beaten by Edward I's troops. Retrace your steps, under the viaduct, turn left into Tamfourhill Road, and left through the kissing gate on the left-hand side of the road.

> ### WHAT TO LOOK FOR ⓘ
> **Water voles** live along the waterways and are often confused with rats. Immortalised as Ratty in *Wind in the Willows*, voles are a threatened species. They're vegetarians, have a round snout, and are more likely to be spotted during the day than rats (which like to search for food at night).

② This takes you to a section of the Roman **Antonine Wall** – there's a deep ditch and a rampart behind it. Walk along here, going parallel with **Tamfourhill Road**. When you reach the point where you can go no further, climb up the bank on the right-hand side and go down the steps to join the road by a kissing gate.

③ Go left to continue along the road – you'll soon see another kissing gate on the left leading you

> ### WHERE TO EAT AND DRINK ⓘ
> The **Union Inn** has a restaurant and beer garden. You can get bar snacks such as filled baguettes, wraps or potato skins or heartier meals like lamb, or trout in lemon butter with almonds. Meals are available both at lunchtime and in the evening. On the other side of Lock 16 is the **Canal Inn**. This doesn't serve food but has lots of atmosphere. You can sit outside on fine days.

> ### WHILE YOU'RE THERE ⓘ
> You pass several sections of the **Antonine Wall** on this walk. It was built in AD 142–3 by Emperor Antonius Pius and stretched for 37 miles (60km), marking the most northerly boundary of the Roman Empire.

to another, much shorter, section of the wall. Leave the wall, rejoin the road and maintain direction to reach a mini-roundabout. Turn left here, along **Maryfield Place**. When you reach the end, join the public footpath signed to the canal tow path and woodland walks. Follow this track as it winds up and over the railway bridge, then on to reach the **Union Canal**.

④ Don't cross the canal but turn right and walk along the tow path. This is a long straight stretch now, popular with local joggers. Eventually you'll reach **Roughcastle tunnel** – but remember that it currently closes at 6PM so as to protect the Wheel from vandalism.

⑤ Walk through the tunnel – it's bright and clean and dry. This will bring you out to the new **Falkirk Wheel** and yet another section of the Antonine Wall. You can walk on as far as the Wheel, then walk down to the visitors' centre at the bottom. Bear right from here to cross the little bridge over the **Forth and Clyde Canal**.

⑥ Turn right now and walk along the tow path. Lots of dog walkers and cyclists come along here (so take care if you are walking with a dog), while people frequently go canoeing along the canal. Keep walking until you come back to **Lock 16**, then turn right and cross the canal again to return to the start of the walk at the **Union Inn**.

A Leisurely Circuit of Culross

An easy walk that ends on the cobbled streets of an historic town, where a prosperous trading history is reflected in the buildings.

•DISTANCE•	3 miles (4.8km)
•MINIMUM TIME•	1hr 30min
•ASCENT / GRADIENT•	180ft (55m) ▲▲ ▲
•LEVEL OF DIFFICULTY•	🚶🚶 🚶 🚶
•PATHS•	Generally firm paths, some muddy woodland tracks
•LANDSCAPE•	Ancient town, fields and woodland
•SUGGESTED MAP•	aqua3 OS Explorer 367 Dunfermline & Kirkcaldy
•START / FINISH•	Grid reference: NS 983859
•DOG FRIENDLINESS•	Can run free on woodland tracks
•PARKING•	Culross West car park
•PUBLIC TOILETS•	By car park in Culross

BACKGROUND TO THE WALK

Walking through Culross is a bit like stepping on to a film set. With its neat cobbled streets and immaculately preserved buildings, it gives you the impression that you've stepped back in time. The pretty little houses, with their red pantiled roofs and crow-stepped gables, give the place a Flemish look – a typical feature of Scottish architecture of this period. Yet despite its neatly manicured appearance, Culross owes its origins to industry – coal mining to be precise.

Monks and Miners

The mining industry was started in the 13th century by the Cistercian monks of Culross Abbey, and a flourishing trade soon developed. Coal production allowed a salt-panning industry to grow up, with fires from inferior quality coal being used to evaporate sea water. By the 16th century Culross was one of the largest ports in Scotland, exporting both coal and salt to the Low Countries and the Baltic. On their return journeys they carried red pantiles as ballast – which were used to give the town's roofs their distinctive appearance. There are reminders of these days throughout the town. The area known as the Sandhaven, for instance, which you pass at the end of this walk, was once the harbour. As you pass it, take a look at the Tron, where officials would weigh export cargoes to assess their tax – you can still see the stone platform that supported the weighing beam.

Culross Palace

Trade brought prosperity to the town, as you can see from the many substantial buildings that dot the streets. Most striking of all is Culross Palace, a beautiful ochre-coloured town house. It was built in 1597 by Sir George Bruce, the local bigwig who owned both the mines and the salt pans – the pine-panelled walls, decorative paintings and period furniture reflect the lifestyle of a rich merchant of the period. If you go on a tour, look out for the Flemish-style paintings on the wooden ceiling in the Painted Chamber.

Eventually the industries in Culross died out and the village went to sleep, its period features preserved like those of an insect trapped in amber. However, in 1923 the palace was bought by the National Trust for Scotland, which then went on to purchase more properties in the village.

As you near the end of this walk, do make time to explore. Walking down the hill you'll pass The House with the Evil Eyes – so named because of the shape of its windows – then the church and the remains of Culross Abbey, before coming into the centre of the village. Look for the street known as The Haggs or Stinking Wynd. If you look carefully you'll see that the centre is higher than the edges. This was 'the crown o' the causie', the place where the local toffs walked. The unfortunate *hoi polloi* had to walk in the gutters – which would have been swimming with – well, you can imagine.

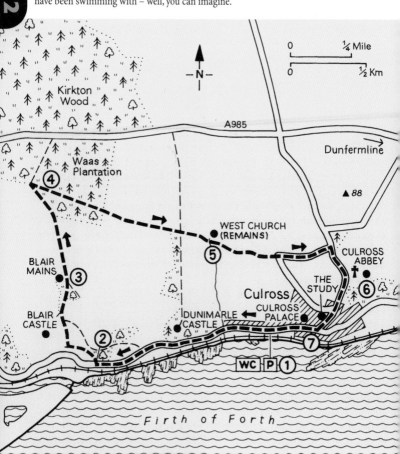

Walk 32 **Directions**

① Turn left out of the car park and walk along the road, with the bay to your left and housing on your right. Continue walking, past some cottages, until you reach the edge of the town. Take care of traffic now as there is no pavement. Pass the entrance to **Dunimarle Castle** on your right and continue until you reach the entrance to **Blair Castle** – now a memorial home for miners.

② Turn right and walk up the tarmac drive (signposted 'private') which is lined with rhododendrons. Walk until you can see the castle on the left. Before you reach it, take the right-hand turning in the trees and follow it as it bears to the right. Continue until you reach **Blair Mains farmhouse** on the left.

WHILE YOU'RE THERE

Dunfermline Abbey, in nearby Dunfermline, dates back to the 11th century. The only remains of the original church are the foundations as it was ravaged by raiders many times. It is the burial place of six Scottish kings, as well as Robert the Bruce who is buried beneath the pulpit.

---

③ Continue following the track, walking under a line of pylons with fields on either side. Walk ahead towards the trees and continue following this track until you reach a metal gate on the left-hand side. Look carefully and you should spot a wooden fence post on the right-hand side, with the words 'West Kirk' and 'grave' painted on it in white. Take the narrow right-hand path immediately before it, which runs through the trees.

④ Follow this path to go through a kissing gate and continue walking ahead, with trees on your left and fields on your right. Go through another kissing gate, and continue in the same direction as the path opens out to a wider, grassy track.

WHERE TO EAT AND DRINK

There's a café in the **Bessie Bar Hall** in the palace where you can get home-made cakes and snacks and hot drinks. Alternatively you can go a little way along the coast to Limekilns to have a drink in the **Ship Inn**, which featured in Robert Louis Stevenson's *Kidnapped*.

When you reach a crossing of paths, continue ahead along a narrow path and walk under a line of pylons. You will soon pass the remains of a church on the left-hand side.

⑤ Continue ahead, past the old cemetery, and walk in the same direction until the track joins a tarmac road. Walk in the same direction until you reach a junction. Turn right here and head downhill – watch out for traffic now as the road can be busy. You will soon reach **Culross Abbey** on the left-hand side.

⑥ It's worth stopping at this point to visit the abbey. You can then continue to walk on downhill, down **Tanhouse Brae,** and will soon reach the **Mercat** ('old Market') **Cross**, with **The Study** on the right-hand side. Continue walking in the same direction, down **Back Causeway**, until you reach the main road.

WHAT TO LOOK FOR

The **Town House** in the Sandhaven was built in 1626 and used to be the seat for local government. The ground floor used to be a prison for debtors, while the attic was used to imprison 'witches'. On one of the houses near by is an elegant wall-mounted sundial – a somewhat unusual feature, given the chilly nature of Scottish summers.

---

⑦ Turn right, walk past the tourist information centre, past **the Tron** (the old burgh weighing machine), then past the large ochre-coloured building on the right, which is **Culross Palace** (► Background to the Walk) . To reach the starting point, continue walking in the same direction – the car park is on the left-hand side, just past the children's play area.

Stirling's Braveheart

Discover the truth about William Wallace on this town trail.

•DISTANCE•	4 miles (6.4km)
•MINIMUM TIME•	2hrs
•ASCENT / GRADIENT•	279ft (85m) ▲▲▲
•LEVEL OF DIFFICULTY•	林 林 林
•PATHS•	Ancient city streets and some rough tracks
•LANDSCAPE•	Bustling little city topped with magnificent castle
•SUGGESTED MAP•	aqua3 OS Explorer 366 Stirling & Ochil Hills West
•START / FINISH•	Grid reference: NS 795933
•DOG FRIENDLINESS•	Mostly on lead, not good for those that dislike crowds
•PARKING•	On streets near TIC or in multi-storey car parks
•PUBLIC TOILETS•	At visitor centre by Castle

BACKGROUND TO THE WALK

To many Scots he is the ultimate hero, a charismatic patriot who died fighting for his country's freedom. To others he is less exalted – an outlaw and murderer. Discovering the truth about William Wallace is not easy, as few contemporary accounts exist – although we can be reasonably assured that he didn't look like Mel Gibson or paint his face with woad.

Wallace's heroic status is immediately obvious on your arrival in Stirling, which is dominated by the enormous monument erected in his memory. He was born at Ellerslie near Kilmarnock (not Elderslie as was originally thought) early in the 1270s (see, even his birth is something of a mystery) and little is known of his early life. He might have remained unknown were it not for the fact that in 1286 the Scottish King, Alexander III, was found dead on the sands at Kinghorn, Fife. His only direct heir was Margaret of Norway – and many powerful Scots did not want a woman on the throne. When Margaret died on her way to Scotland, the succession was plunged into further confusion. The only likely contestants were John Balliol and Robert Bruce. Edward I of England was asked to advise, chose Balliol, and then exerted his authority by demanding revenues from Scotland. Balliol later infuriated Edward by signing a treaty with England's enemy, France, and Edward retaliated by sacking Berwick in 1296, slaughtering thousands. The Scots began to resist, Balliol was deposed as king, and the Wars of Independence began.

Wallace Wages War

Wallace joined the struggle. In 1297 he killed the English Sheriff of Lanark and led a number of attacks on English forces. Later that year he won the battle that was to make his reputation, defeating Edward's army at Stirling Bridge. Wallace's forces killed thousands of English and Welsh troops, driving the wounded into the marshes to drown. Wallace now had considerable power. Faced with the possibility of food shortages in Scotland, he ordered an invasion of northern England to plunder food. Many villagers were murdered, churches were burned and over 700 villages destroyed.

In 1298 Wallace was made Guardian of Scotland, but was defeated by Edward I later that year at the Battle of Falkirk. He resigned the Guardianship and travelled to Rome to enlist support from the Pope for the restoration of Balliol as king. Back in Scotland, he continually refused to accept Edward as King of Scotland and was eventually captured and taken prisoner in 1305 (some say he was betrayed by Scots). He was executed at Smithfield in London (the torture of being hung, drawn and quartered was invented for him) and immediately became a martyr for Scottish independence.

Walk 33 Directions

① From the tourist information centre on **Dumbarton Road**, cross the road and turn left. Walk past the statue of Robert Burns then, just before the **Albert Halls**, turn right

and walk back on yourself. Just past the statue of Rob Roy, turn left and join the **Back Wall**.

② Follow this path uphill, with the old town wall on your right. Go up the flight of steps that takes you on to the **Upper Back Wall**. It's a steady

Walk 33

climb now, up past **Lady's Rock** – where ladies of the castle once sat to watch medieval tournaments – and on past the **Star Pyramid**, a triangular cone incongruously situated by a graveyard.

③ Continue following the path uphill to reach **Stirling Castle**. Take the path running downhill just to the side of the visitor centre, so that the castle is on your left. At the bottom go left and walk to the cemetery. Turn right and follow the path to the other side of the cemetery. Bear right and go through the gap in the wall.

> **WHILE YOU'RE THERE** ⓘ
> **Cambuskenneth Abbey** was founded by Augustinian canons in 1147 for David I. Although the only surviving feature is the 14th-century belfry, it was once one of Scotland's richest abbeys. Robert the Bruce held his parliament here in 1326 and James III and his wife, Margaret of Denmark, are buried in the grounds.

④ Follow the track downhill on to **Gowan Hill**. There are several branching tracks but you continue on the main path – heading for the cannons on the hill ahead. You'll come down to a wider grassy track, then climb uphill to the **Beheading Stone**. Retrace your steps to the wide track and follow it to the road.

⑤ Turn right along **Lower Bridge Street**, then fork right into **Upper Bridge Street**. Continue ahead, then turn right down **Barn Road**. Follow it uphill, then go left at the top. Eventually you'll pass the **Castle Esplanade**, followed by **Argyll's Lodging**, and will reach a junction.

⑥ Turn left, passing **Hermann's Restaurant** and the **Mercat Cross**. Turn right at the bottom down **Bow Street**, then left along **Baker Street**. When you reach **Friars Street** (which is pedestrianised), turn left and walk down to the end.

⑦ Turn right now, then first left to reach the station. Turn left, then right over the bridge, continuing to reach the riverside. Maintain direction and join **Abbey Road**. Bear left at the end, go right over the footbridge and continue along South Street, turning right at the end to visit the remains of **Cambuskenneth Abbey**.

⑧ Retrace your steps now, over the footbridge and back to the station. Turn right at the station, then left at the top to pass the **Thistle Shopping Centre**. Continue along **Port Street**, then turn right and walk along **Dumbarton Road** to the start.

> **WHERE TO EAT AND DRINK** ⓘ
> You've got plenty of choice in Stirling. **La Ciocare** is a 50s-style cool green Italian bar/bistro which serves ice creams, cakes, frothy cappuccinos and pizza. Just round the corner there's the **Barnton Bar and Bistro**, which has murky old-fashioned appeal and is popular with those seeking all-day breakfasts and snacks. For sandwiches, cakes and baked potatoes try **Darnley Coffee House** – said to have been the home of Lord Darnley, Mary, Queen of Scots' husband.

> **WHAT TO LOOK FOR** ⓘ
> It's worth breaking your walk to visit impressive **Stirling Castle**, which was the favourite residence of most of the Stuart monarchs. You can see the interior of the Chapel Royal, which was built by James VI in 1594 for the baptism of his son, and also the 16th-century kitchens which have been restored. You can also see the palace, where Mary, Queen of Scots lived until she left Scotland for France.

Walk **34**

And Over Stirling Bridge

An extension taking you up to the magnificent Wallace Monument.
See map and information panel for Walk 33

•DISTANCE•	6 miles (9.7km)
•MINIMUM TIME•	3hrs
•ASCENT / GRADIENT•	295ft (90m) ▲▲▲
•LEVEL OF DIFFICULTY•	🚶🚶🚶

Walk 34 Directions (Walk 33 option)

From Point ⑤, you take the road that runs ahead of you – this is **Union Street**. Walk to the end to reach a roundabout. Turn left now, then go through the underpass which takes you to the other side of the busy road. Bear right and walk over the attractive bridge ahead of you – this is **Old Stirling Bridge**, the site of William Wallace's famous victory.

Once over the bridge, bear right to reach the main road (Point Ⓐ). It's a long walk now alongside a busy road – it's difficult to imagine what ancient Stirling was like with the cars whizzing past you. However, you'll eventually come to a roundabout (Point Ⓑ) where you turn right to walk along **Alloa Road**. Just a short distance along on your left is a park and a children's play area. Cross this and you will soon spot some steps in the woods ahead of you (Point Ⓒ).

You can now climb these steps to the top of the crag to reach the **Wallace Monument** – if you want to climb the monument itself you'll have to pay, but the views on a clear

day are great. Walk back down the steps now, across the park, then turn left at the road. Walk a short distance until you reach **Ladysneuk Road** (Point Ⓓ). Turn right and walk down here. You'll have to go over a level crossing so cross it with care, then continue along the road. At the bottom, on your left-hand side, you will come to the remains of **Cambuskenneth Abbey**. After visiting this, rejoin the main walk at Point ⑧.

To return to town, walk along **South Street**, over the footbridge, then bear left and sharp right to walk along **Abbey Road**, then **Shore Road** and up over the bridge over the railway. Turn left, walk to the station and continue with Point ⑧ of the main walk.

WHILE YOU'RE THERE
The **Battle of Bannockburn** (1314) is one of the most famous battles in Scottish history and the battle site is not far from Stirling. It was the scene of Scotland's greatest victory over the English, when Robert the Bruce defeated the army of Edward II. It was a victory that was to unite the Scots and led to the Declaration of Arbroath in 1320 – a demand for independence and freedom from English rule. You can visit the heritage centre here and see the statue erected to Bruce.

A Darn Walk from Dunblane

An easy linear riverside walk with memories of Robert Louis Stevenson.

Walk 35

•DISTANCE•	3 miles (4.8km)
•MINIMUM TIME•	1hr 30min
•ASCENT / GRADIENT•	33ft (10m)
•LEVEL OF DIFFICULTY•	
•PATHS•	Firm tracks and pavements throughout
•LANDSCAPE•	Quiet riverbanks and small towns, plus grand cathedral
•SUGGESTED MAP•	aqua3 OS Explorer 366 Stirling & Ochil Hills West
•START•	Grid reference: NS 781009
•FINISH•	Grid reference: NS 785977
•DOG FRIENDLINESS•	Good, can run free for much of walk
•PARKING•	By station in Dunblane
•PUBLIC TOILETS•	Near station in Dunblane

Walk 35 Directions

This easy walk takes you from Dunblane to Bridge of Allan, following an ancient track beside the Allan Water known as the Darn Road. This is an ancient route and gets its name from the old Gaelic 'Dobhran' or Water Road.

From the station, walk past the **Dunblane Hotel** to go over the bridge, then turn left down **Mill Row**. You now follow the wide track that takes you beside the **Allan Water**. You'll pass a bridge on the left-hand side, and will then continue to walk under a railway bridge. Follow the path until you reach another bridge, where you cross a small burn and take the path that bears right, passing a children's play area. Follow this path as it brings you up to the railway line, then bears left so that you're parallel with the track. You'll soon reach some steps on the right-hand side, which take you down to a bridge and across the railway. Your path

now continues ahead, taking you over rough ground that in summer is ablaze with pink rosebay willowherb and golden ragwort. Follow the main track to a fingerpost, signed 'Ashfield 1'. You turn right here, following the edge of the burn until you reach a crossing of tracks. Turn right here and cross the burn, following the track as it now swings up to the road. When you reach the road, turn right. You'll now pass some attractive old weaver's cottages, reminders of the weaving industry that was once so important to this area. Bear left at the end of the road and walk straight down to reach **Dunblane Cathedral**. This was built in the 13th century and is

---

WHILE YOU'RE THERE ⓘ

Sheriffmuir, near Dunblane, was the site of a battle in 1715, when Jacobite supporters fought government troops on the crest of the hill near the Gathering Stone, a fallen prehistoric standing stone. The Jacobites were driven down to the Allan Water and prevented from marching into Stirling and seizing the castle.

noted for its fine stained-glass windows and carved wood. Most of the medieval stained glass in Scotland was destroyed after the Reformation, so that in the cathedral is of more recent origin. Some of the windows were created by C E Kempe, who is considered one of the finest Victorian stained-glass artists.

> **WHERE TO EAT AND DRINK** ℹ
> The best choice is in Bridge of Allan. The 50s-style **Allan Water Café** is very popular with locals for its ice creams and meals such as fish and chips. You can also try the **Queens Hotel**, which serves things like club sandwiches and baked potatoes, as well as more substantial meals like mussels and pasta.

After visiting the cathedral, continue walking down to join the **High Street** and walk up to the **Stirling Arms Hotel**. Walk ahead, keeping the hotel on your right, and go up to reach the main road. Cross the road with care, then take the track almost opposite the police station – it's signposted 'Bridge of Allan 2½'. You're now on the **Darn Road**. It's a straight track and easy to follow. You'll pass a golf course on the left-hand side and will then go through a wooden gate which takes you into woodland. Eventually you'll come to a footbridge over the **Wharry Burn**, and then a signpost where you follow the signs for Bridge of Allan. You'll now see the river on your right-hand side. Ignore the footbridge on the right and continue ahead. You'll soon come to a cave on the left, said by some to be the inspiration for Ben Gunn's cave in Robert Louis Stevenson's *Treasure Island* (1883). Stevenson is one of Scotland's great literary figures and is particularly remembered for his gripping

adventure stories. His childhood holidays were spent in Dunblane and he mentions the Allan Water in *Kidnapped* (1886). He later travelled widely and wrote many travel books. He suffered from poor health and moved to Samoa in the hope of benefiting from the climate. He died in 1894, aged just 44.

After this you'll come to some steps, which take you higher above the water. Follow the path downhill and over a footbridge with green railings. Continue to follow the track as it takes you beside pasturelands and then houses on the left-hand side, before eventually bringing you up to the main road. Turn right now and walk into **Bridge of Allan**. Turn left and walk along **Henderson Street**, the bustling main street which is lined with shops and eating places. At **Fountain Road** turn right. You will soon come to **Holy Trinity Church** on the right-hand side, noted for its associations with Charles Rennie Mackintosh. Walk down to the fountain, then turn right along **Union Street** – almost doubling back on yourself. You'll pass some unusual cottages on the right-hand side. Follow this road as it bears round to the right and back on to **Henderson Street**. You now turn left and walk ahead to cross over the bridge, then turn left down **Inverallan Road** to the station to catch the train back to Dunblane.

> **WHAT TO LOOK FOR** ℹ
> **Bridge of Allan** was once a small spa town where wealthy people came to drink the curative waters. A large number of properties were built to cater for these visitors, giving the town its prosperous feel. Those taking the 'cure' would drink four pints (2.3l) of the water each morning , then relax and explore.

The Romance of Rob Roy in Callander

Steep wooded paths lead you through the crags for superb views of the Trossachs.

•DISTANCE•	3 miles (4.8km)
•MINIMUM TIME•	2hrs 15min
•ASCENT / GRADIENT•	896ft (273m) ▲▲▲
•LEVEL OF DIFFICULTY•	🏃 🏃 🏃
•PATHS•	Forest tracks and some rocky paths
•LANDSCAPE•	Mixed woodlands, great views of hills and lochs
•SUGGESTED MAP•	aqua3 OS Explorer 365 The Trossachs
•START / FINISH•	Grid reference: NN 625079
•DOG FRIENDLINESS•	Can run free – steep climb and crags might not suit some
•PARKING•	Riverside car park
•PUBLIC TOILETS•	Callander

BACKGROUND TO THE WALK

A s you climb through the trees and scramble over the rocks above Callander, it is easy to imagine yourself back in the late 17th century, when Rob Roy and his clansmen lived as outlaws in the heart of the Trossachs. His name has for centuries been tied up with myth and legend, and has inspired many authors and film makers – including Sir Walter Scott, who wrote a romantic account of his life in his eponymous novel of 1818. For some Rob Roy is a Highland hero, for others a notorious cattle thief – whatever the truth behind the myth, he is certainly one of the most colourful characters in Scottish history.

The Wicked Clan Gregor

Rob Roy (the Gaelic for Red Robert) was more properly known as Robert MacGregor. Born in 1671, he was the son of Donald MacGregor of Glengyle. This clan – the 'wicked Clan Gregor' – had been outlawed in 1603, and was known as 'the nameless clan' as they were even forbidden to use their name. The MacGregors had a violent reputation, as they defended their lands and cattle vigorously against assaults from neighbouring clans – which included the rival Campbells, who acted as government agents. Rob Roy, living as a cattle herder in Balquhidder, kept an armed band of men to protect him and his cattle – and extended their services to neighbours who paid him protection money. He began to extend his influence and eventually made a claim to be the chief of the clan.

In 1712 Rob Roy borrowed money from the Duke of Montrose for a speculative cattle deal, and suffered heavy losses, which caused a terrible rift between them. His lands were seized, his properties plundered and his wife and children were turned out of their home in the middle of winter. These were already troubled times, for the Jacobite rebellion had begun in 1689 and there were frequent battles between government forces and the supporters of James. Rob Roy, who had fought on the Jacobite side at Sheriffmuir, now gathered his clansmen and took revenge on the Duke of Montrose, who was a powerful supporter of the government.

Loved by the Good

As a result, Rob Roy was outlawed and stories began to appear about his dramatic escapes from his pursuers. He even began to be seen as a sort of Robin Hood figure, generously helping the poor by stealing from the rich. Local people would help him and warn him if troops were in the area.

However, Rob Roy's luck didn't last – he was eventually captured in 1727 and was sentenced to transportation. He was later pardoned and went back to Balquhidder, where he seems to have settled down and lived quietly for the rest of his life. He died in 1734 and is buried in Balquhidder churchyard.

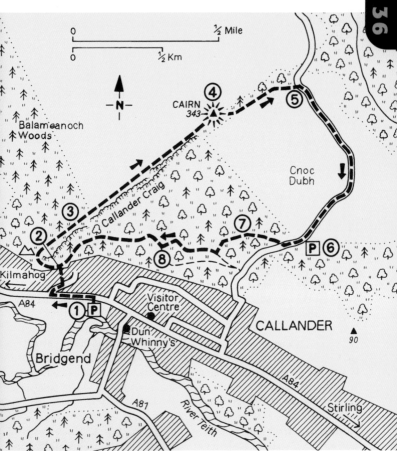

Walk 36 Directions

① From the **Riverside car park**, walk back to the main road, then turn left. Follow this, then turn right along **Tulliepan Crescent**. Just in front of the new housing estate, turn left and follow the wide track. Where the track splits, take the path on the left that is signposted 'The Crags'.

② Your path now winds steeply uphill through the trees and can get slippery if there's been a lot of rain. Keep following the path and cross a footbridge. Climb to reach a wall on

Walk 36

the left-hand side, after which your path narrows. Follow it to pass a large boulder.

③ Continue following the path, which eventually bears left, up some steps to a fence. Cross another footbridge, scramble over some rocks and go through a metal kissing gate. You eventually come to a **memorial cairn**, created in 1897 for Queen Victoria's Diamond Jubilee. On a clear day there are stunning, panoramic views of the surrounding countryside.

④ Leaving the cairn, your path now begins to wind downhill. It's rocky in places and you'll need to take some care as you descend. Eventually you'll spot the road through the trees. Turn right into the trees and walk down to join it.

⑤ Turn right along the road – you'll see the Wallace Monument near Stirling in the far distance. You'll soon pass a sign on the right-hand side for the **Red Well**, where the water runs a distinctly reddish colour owing to the presence of iron traces in the local rock. Continue until you reach a car park on your left. You can make a detour here to see the **Bracklyn Falls**.

⑥ After the car park, stay on the road for about 100yds (91m), then turn right to climb some wooden steps – they're signposted 'The

> **WHILE YOU'RE THERE** ℹ
> In the centre of Callender is the **Rob Roy and Trossachs Visitor Centre**. There's an audio-visual presentation which takes you through the lands he once lived in, and tells you the story of his life. Rob Roy and his clansmen, you'll discover, were known as the 'Children of the Mist' – as they would appear suddenly out of the mist to steal cattle or collect their protection money.

Crags Upper Wood Walk', but the sign faces away from you. Walk past a small building, cross a little footbridge and walk to a crossing of footpaths.

⑦ Turn left for a few paces, then turn right. Continue walking through the woods, cross a footbridge and, when you reach a wider, slate-covered track, turn right and walk uphill. At the end of the track, turn left and walk downhill until you reach a wooden seat and a footbridge.

⑧ Take the path that runs to the right of the seat (don't cross the footbridge). Follow the path as it runs downhill and takes you back to the place at which you entered the woods. Turn right, then go left along the main road and walk back into **Callander** to the car park at the start of the walk.

> **WHERE TO EAT AND DRINK** ℹ
> There are several cafés and pubs in Callander. **Dun Whinny's**, on Bridge Street, serves a good selection of toasted sandwiches, light meals and home baking as well as foamy cappuccinos. It can get busy so you can also try **Pip's Coffee House** near by. A few miles north at Kilmahog is the **Lade Inn**.

> **WHAT TO LOOK FOR** ℹ
> In Callander you won't be able to escape the **Highland kitsch** that seems to accompany every Scottish tourist attraction, but its origins are at least ancient. The word **clan** comes from the Gaelic word 'clann'. This originally meant 'children' but gradually came to be used to refer to 'kindred'. The earliest clan was Clann Duib, or Clan Duff. They were the ruling family of Fife. The head of the clan was referred to as MacDuib, or MacDuff.

Academic Traditions at St Andrews

On this easy town trail, discover an ancient university, which observes some very strange traditions.

Walk 37

•DISTANCE•	4½ miles (7.2km)
•MINIMUM TIME•	2hrs
•ASCENT / GRADIENT•	33ft (10m) ▲▲ ▲ ▲
•LEVEL OF DIFFICULTY•	🚶 🚶 🚶
•PATHS•	Ancient streets and golden sands
•LANDSCAPE•	Historic university town and windy seascapes
•SUGGESTED MAP•	aqua3 OS Explorer 371 St Andrews & East Fife
•START / FINISH•	Grid reference: NO 506170
•DOG FRIENDLINESS•	Can run free on beach – may not like busy streets
•PARKING•	Free parking along The Scores, otherwise several car parks
•PUBLIC TOILETS•	Several close to beach

BACKGROUND TO THE WALK

St Andrews is famous for two things – as the home of golf and of an ancient university. A small town on the Fife coast, it has an atmosphere all its own and feels quite unlike any other town in Scotland. Its isolated location – there is no station here – is considered to be one of the reasons why Prince William chose to study here – a decision that prompted a massive increase in applications, largely from young women hoping to nab themselves a future king.

Reasons for Raisins

The university was established in 1410 and is the oldest in Scotland, and third oldest in Britain – after Oxford and Cambridge. The first faculties established here were theology, canon law, civil law, medicine and arts – with theology being of particular importance. In medieval times students could enter the university as young as 13, and a system of seniority soon arose among the student body. New students were known as bejaunus, from the French 'bec-jaune' or fledgling, and were initiated into the fraternity on Raisin Monday, when they were expected to produce a pound of raisins in return for a cheeky receipt. The tradition persists today, with bejants, as they are now known (females are bejantines), being taken under the wings of older students who become their 'academic parents'. On Raisin Sunday, in November, academic 'fathers' take their charges out to get thoroughly drunk. The next day, Raisin Monday, the 'mothers' put them in fancy dress before they and their hangovers congregate in St Salvator's quad for a flour and egg fight.

Elizabeth Garrett, the first woman in Britain to qualify as a doctor, was allowed to matriculate at St Andrews in 1862 but was then rejected after the Senate declared her enrolment illegal. Following this the university made efforts to encourage the education of women, who were finally allowed full membership of the university in 1892. In 1866 Elizabeth Garrett established a dispensary for women in London, which later became the famous Elizabeth Garrett Anderson Hospital.

Treasured Traditions

The university is proud of its traditions and, as you walk around the streets today, you might well spot students wearing their distinctive scarlet gowns. These were introduced after about 1640 and some say they were brightly coloured so that students could be spotted when entering the local brothels. They are made of a woolly fabric with a velvet yoke. First-year students wear them over both shoulders, gradually casting them off each year, until in their fourth and final year the gowns hang down, almost dragging behind them.

Other university traditions include a Sunday walk along the pier after church, which continued until the pier was closed for repair, and a mass dawn swim in the sea on May morning (1 May). Given the particularly icy nature of the waters, this is not an activity to be attempted by the faint-hearted.

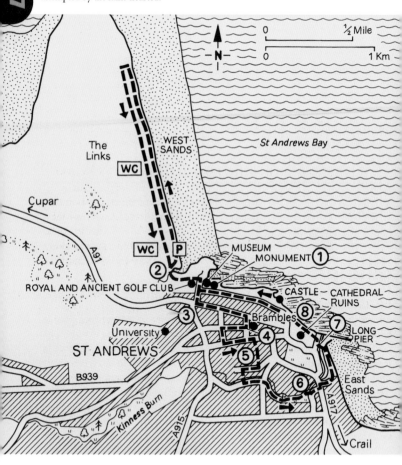

Walk 37 Directions

① With the **Martyrs Monument** on **The Scores** in front of you, walk left past the bandstand. At the road turn right, walk to the **British Golf Museum**, then turn left. Pass the clubhouse of the **Royal and Ancient Golf Club** on your left, then bear right at the burn to reach the beach.

② Your route now takes you along the **West Sands**. Walk as far as you

Walk 37

choose, then either retrace your steps along the beach or take one of the paths through the dunes to join the tarmac road. Walk back to the **Golf Museum**, then turn right and walk to the main road.

③ Turn left along the road and walk to **St Salvator's College**. Take a peek through the archway at the serene quadrangle – and look at the initials PH in the cobbles outside. They commemorate Patrick Hamilton, who was martyred here in 1528 – they say students who tread on the site will fail their exams. Now cross over and walk to the end of **College Street**.

④ Turn right and walk along **Market Street**. At the corner turn left along **Bell Street**, then left again on **South Street**. Just after you pass **Church Street**, cross over into the quadrangle of **St Mary's College**. Join the path on the right and walk up to reach **Queen's Terrace**.

⑤ Turn right to reach the red-brick house, then left down steeply sloping **Dempster Terrace**. At the end cross the burn, turn left and

walk to the main road. Cross over and walk along **Glebe Road**. At the park, take the path that bears left, walk past the play area and up to **Woodburn Terrace**.

⑥ Turn left to join **St Mary Street**, turn left again, then go right along **Woodburn Place**. You'll now bear left beside the beach. You'll get good views of the Long Pier, where students traditionally walked on Sunday mornings. Cross the footbridge and join the road.

⑦ Bear right for a few paces, then ascend the steps on the left. These bring you up to the remains of a church and on to the famous ruined **cathedral**. A gate in the wall on the left gives access to the site.

⑧ Your route then takes you past the ancient castle on the right. A former palace/fortress, it was at the forefront of the Reformation – John Knox preached here. Pass the **Castle Visitor Centre**, then continue along **The Scores** to return to the start.

A Fishy Trail in Fife

A linear coastal walk through the villages of Fife's East Neuk.

Walk 38

•DISTANCE•	4 miles (6.4km)
•MINIMUM TIME•	1hrs 30min
•ASCENT / GRADIENT•	49ft (15m) ▲ ▲ ▲
•LEVEL OF DIFFICULTY•	🚶🚶 🚶🚶 🚶🚶
•PATHS•	Well-marked coastal path, 3 stiles
•LANDSCAPE•	Picturesque fishing villages and extensive sea views
•SUGGESTED MAP•	aqua3 OS Explorer 371 St Andrews & East Fife
•START•	Grid reference: NO 613077
•FINISH•	Grid reference: NO 569034
•DOG FRIENDLINESS•	Good, but keep on lead near cattle
•PARKING•	On street in Crail
•PUBLIC TOILETS•	Route passes plenty both in Crail and Anstruther

BACKGROUND TO THE WALK

Scotland's James II described the East Neuk (nook) of Fife as 'a fringe of gold on a beggar's mantle.' This corner of the east coast is dotted with picturesque fishing villages, which nestle close together yet retain their own distinctive character.

Crail, where your trail begins, is perhaps the prettiest village, with a neat little harbour, which attracts many artists and photographers. It was once the largest fishmarket in Europe and, like all the East Neuk villages, used to trade with the Low Countries and Scandinavia; you can see the Dutch influence in the houses with their crow-stepped gables and pantiled roofs. Today Crail's main industry is tourism.

Further down the coast is Anstruther (known locally as 'Enster'), the largest and busiest of all the villages and home of the local lifeboat. Fishing has always been the focus of life here. The village was the capital of the Scottish herring trade and the harbour was once so busy that you could cross it by stepping over the boats. Look at the houses as you pass and you'll see that many of them have spacious lofts with a pulley outside – designed to store fishing gear and provide an area for mending the nets.

Fishing dominated the lives of people in the past and each of the East Neuk villages was a closely knit community. It was rare for people to marry outside their own village and women were as heavily involved in the work as the men. They prepared the fish, baited the hooks, mended the nets and took the fish to market for sale, carrying enormous baskets of herrings on their backs for miles. They also used to carry their husbands out to sea on their backs so that they could board their boats without getting wet.

Fishing has always had considerable dangers and many local superstitions are attached to the industry. Women are never allowed aboard when a boat is working, and it is considered unlucky to utter the word 'minister' on a boat – he had to be referred to as 'the fellow with the white throat' or 'man in the black coat' instead. Other words that have to be avoided are 'pig', 'rat' and 'salmon'. These are known as 'curlytail', 'lang-tail' and 'red fish' (or 'silver beastie') respectively. If these forbidden words were spoken on a fishing boat the men would cry 'cauld airn' (cold iron) and grab hold of the nearest piece of iron – even if it was just a nail in a shoe. It's the equivalent of touching wood and is meant to break the bad luck.

Walk 38 Directions

① From the tourist information centre in **Crail**, walk down **Tolbooth Wynd**. At the end turn right and continue to the garage, where you bear left (a sign says 'no vehicular access to harbour'). You'll now walk by the old castle wall to a lookout point, which gives you a good view of the picturesque harbour. Bear right and walk on to the **High Street**.

② Turn left and walk along the road, passing the two white beacons, which help guide boats into the harbour. Turn left and walk down **West Braes**, following the signs for the Coast Path. When you reach **Osbourne Terrace** bear slightly left, go down some steps, through a kissing gate and on to a grassy track by the shore.

③ From here you follow the path as it hugs the shoreline. You should soon see cormorants perched on rocks to your left and will also get views of the Isle of May. Go down some steps, over a slightly boggy area, and continue walking until you reach two derelict cottages – an area known as **The Pans**.

④ Walk past the cottages and continue along the shore, then hop over a stone stile. You'll now pass flat rocks on the left, which are covered with interesting little rock pools. Cross the burn by the footbridge – you'll now be able to see the Bass Rock and Berwick Law on your left and the village of Anstruther ahead, and will soon reach some caves.

⑤ Pass the caves, then cross a little stone stile on the left-hand side and go over a footbridge. Your track is narrower now and takes you past fields on the right, then some maritime grasses on the left. Big

WHAT TO LOOK FOR ⓘ
The **Lifeboat Station** is often open to visitors. The local lifeboat, manned by RNLI volunteers, is regularly called into service and over 300 lives have been saved since one was first established here. The harbour is drained at low tide, so to be launched, it has to be pulled from the shed by a tractor and dragged to the water.

stepping stones now take you to another stile, which you climb over to reach **Caiplie**.

⑥ Go through the kissing gate by the houses, follow the wide grassy track, then go through another kissing gate to walk past a field. The path now runs past a free-range pig farm and up to a caravan park.

WHILE YOU'RE THERE ⓘ
The **Scottish Fisheries Museum** opposite the Lifeboat Station is full of information on the local fishing industry and tells its story from the earliest times to the present day. There are models of fishing boats and some old vessels in the former boatyard. You can also see a reconstruction of a fisherman's cottage and learn about the life of the fisherfolk.

⑦ You now continue along the shore, following the tarmac track to reach a play area and war memorial on the right. Maintain direction now as you enter the village of Cellardyke – often known as **Anstruther Easter** – and continue to reach the harbour. Pass the harbour and **The Haven** restaurant and continue walking along **John Street** and then **James Street**.

⑧ At the end of James Street maintain direction, then follow the road as it bends down to the left. You'll walk past a guiding beacon and will come into Anstruther's busy little harbour. You can now either walk back to **Crail** or take the bus which leaves from the harbour.

WHERE TO EAT AND DRINK ⓘ
There is plenty of choice in Anstruther. Try **Anstruther Fish Bar**, on Shore Street by the harbour. **Brattisanis**, also by the harbour, sells great ice creams, while the **Ship Inn** sells bar meals. For more substantial meals, try the **Dreel Tavern**.

And on to be Inspired by Pittenweem

An extension to a busy fishing village where artists abound.
See map and information panel for Walk 38

•DISTANCE•	1 mile (1.6km)
•MINIMUM TIME•	30min
•ASCENT / GRADIENT•	49ft (15m)
•LEVEL OF DIFFICULTY•	

Walk 39 Directions (Walk 38 option)

From the **Lifeboat Station** at the end of Point ⑧ on the Walk 38, continue walking around Anstruther harbour to reach **Rodger Street** (Point Ⓐ). Cross over the road and maintain your direction to follow the cobbled street ahead. Follow this as it bears right, then turn left at the road. Walk along the road now, past the **Smugglers' Inn**, then bear right at the house covered in shells, decorated in this way by its Victorian owner.

You'll walk past the **Dreel Burn**. This was regularly used by local smugglers, who transported tobacco, cloth, sugar and wine up the burn to trade in Fife, and smuggled linen and coal out.

A plaque at the nearby Dreel Tavern states that James V was carried across this burn by a stout woman when he was travelling incognito through Fife – the local equivalent of Sir Walter Raleigh throwing his cloak over a puddle for Elizabeth I, I suppose.

Follow the road round **Dreelside**, then turn left just past the **Craws Nest Hotel** (Point Ⓑ). Walk to the end of this road, bear right at the end and walk around the edge of the golf course. You'll soon pass a war memorial on the right-hand side and will then continue following the Fife Coast Path which runs round the edge of the greens – take care in case of stray golf balls.

Eventually you reach some stone steps, which you climb up to a seat (Point Ⓒ). Here you bear left with the path, past a field and up to the outskirts of the village. Walk past the children's play area, then bear left at the end and walk downhill to reach **Pittenweem harbour**.

This is a busy little place, dominated by the fish market – the village is the hub of the local fishing industry. You can buy fresh fish here to take home, browse round the art shop where paintings by local artists are on sale, or stop for a drink and a snack at the **Larachmhor pub**. Pittenweem has a reputation as a home and inspiration for artists and holds an Arts Festival every August. To catch the bus back to **Crail**, walk up from the harbour to the main road.

Reclaimed Lochore

Walk through an area that was once the heart of the local mining industry.

Walk 40

•DISTANCE•	3 miles (4.8km)
•MINIMUM TIME•	1hr 15min
•ASCENT / GRADIENT•	66ft (20m)
•LEVEL OF DIFFICULTY•	
•PATHS•	Firm grassy paths and tarmac tracks, 3 stiles
•LANDSCAPE•	Tranquil loch and mixed woodland
•SUGGESTED MAP•	aqua3 OS Explorer 367 Dunfermline & Kirkcaldy
•START / FINISH•	Grid reference: NS 170962
•DOG FRIENDLINESS•	Good, but must stay on lead in some sections
•PARKING•	Lochore Park Centre
•PUBLIC TOILETS•	Lochore Park Centre

Walk 40 Directions

This easy circuit of Lochore introduces you to an area that provides an excellent example of land reclamation. This is essentially an artificial landscape, for the whole area was once at the heart of the coal mining industry. Large numbers of pits here produced very high-quality coal, which was important to Scotland's industrial success. It was hard, dirty work, which once involved the whole family. Men dug the coal from the ground, while women and children worked on the surface. Women would carry the coal to the surface – and the loads were so heavy that it sometimes took two men to lift the basket on to their backs.

From the **Park Centre car park**, walk towards the loch, bear left in the direction of the green, outdoor pursuits building, then follow the sign to join the footpath that runs round the loch. When you get to the footbridge on your right, cross over and walk through a small patch of woodland. When you reach the wide track, turn right then go through the metal kissing gate. You're now walking on grass beside the loch, and although it's an indistinct track it's obvious where you should be going.

As you walk you'll pass gorse bushes and reed beds – and in summer you may spot dainty harebells too. Harebells are also known as Scottish bluebells and like to grow on poor soils. Your path eventually becomes a stone track and then gets craggy in places. Go through a kissing gate, then pass a copse on your left to walk near an island in the lake. The islands are named Moss, Tod and Whaup, taken from old local dialect

WHILE YOU'RE THERE ⓘ
Ravenscraig Castle, which is near the Fife town of Kirkcaldy, is a picturesque ruin on the coast. It is said to be the first castle in Britain that was designed to be defended against cannon fire. Steps near the castle lead down to the beach – if you count, there should be 39. They are said to have inspired John Buchan's famous adventure story.

Walk 40

words for wetlands, fox and curlew respectively. Your way now takes you over three stiles (they're dog-friendly ones) and on to a firm track that leads through the woods.

Lochore was originally a boggy meadow, and with the advent of mining became badly scarred by coal 'bings' or spoil heaps, which covered the ground. When the last coal mine closed down in 1967, a programme of reclamation began. One million trees were planted and a huge effort was made to turn the land into an area that could be enjoyed by the local community, who suffered badly after the loss of the mining jobs. The lake was created and gradually wildlife was coaxed into the area.

WHERE TO EAT AND DRINK

The **Park Centre** at Lochore has a small café serving soup and light meals such as baked potatoes and fish and chips, as well as hot drinks and biscuits. It's open from 10:30AM to 3PM. If it's a fine day, you can take your own food and have a picnic by the lochside.

You'll soon come to a footbridge on your right, which you cross – you can make a short detour if you like by following the track ahead to visit the bird hide. Follow the obvious track (there's a lovely smell of wild thyme in the summer) and the path will then open out on the left-hand side. Go through the metal kissing gate, then turn right to follow the tarmac track. When you reach a fork, a path goes left to **Harran Hill Wood**, which is noted for its carpet of bluebells in spring. This wood has an extensive history and may even have existed since the last ice age. The bluebells, together with the dog's mercury that is also found here, are considered good indicators

of ancient woodland. Dog's mercury has male and female flowers on separate plants. It flowers in spring and is poisonous. Wildlife species that live here include wood mice, woodcock and tawny owls. Woodcocks nest on the forest floor, their plumage cleverly disguising them as a bundle of dead leaves. You continue ahead. If you do this walk in the summer you might well notice hundreds of tiny frogs hopping across the path. Although known as the 'common' frog, they are anything but these days, as their numbers have decreased enormously in recent years. Not only do they suffer predation by large numbers of species, ranging from hedgehogs to herons, their habitats have also declined owing to increased drainage of wetlands.

When the path divides again, turn right to reach the water's edge. (Alternatively you can keep to the tarmac track, which is the old **Pit Road**. If you do this, follow the track to a car park, then turn right to walk back to the visitors' centre.) You now walk round the edge of the loch, following the obvious track by the water until you reach the **visitors' centre** and your starting point. The loch is used today for a variety of water sports such as canoeing, kayaking and dinghy sailing. You'll notice winding gear that once served the mines that covered this area.

WHAT TO LOOK FOR

You might notice some clumps of **wild thyme**. This aromatic plant gets tiny purple flowers from May through to August. It can be used in cooking, but you need to use more of it than the variety you grow in your garden as it has a milder flavour.

Along the Tay to Scone

A town trail of Perth with views over Scotland's ancient capital.

·DISTANCE·	4 miles (6.4km)
·MINIMUM TIME·	1hr 30min
·ASCENT / GRADIENT·	Negligible
·LEVEL OF DIFFICULTY·	
·PATHS·	City streets and wide firm tracks
·LANDSCAPE·	Historic city and wide, lazy river
·SUGGESTED MAP·	aqua3 OS Explorer 369 Perth & Kinross
·START / FINISH·	Grid reference: NO 114237
·DOG FRIENDLINESS·	They'll enjoy river but might not like busy streets
·PARKING·	On street in Perth
·PUBLIC TOILETS·	Off Kinnoull Street in Perth

BACKGROUND TO THE WALK

An ancient description of one of Scotland's most potent symbols – the Stone of Scone, also known as the Stone of Destiny – reads: 'No king was ever wont to reign in Scotland unless he had first sat upon this Stone at Scone.' Scone Palace, of which you get excellent views on this walk, was the crowning place of Scottish kings, including Macbeth and Robert the Bruce. The stone, which was placed on Moot Hill, by the palace, served as their throne – until it was stolen. The last monarch to be crowned on the Moot Hill was Charles II in 1651 – he was recognised as King in Scotland before he was restored to the throne in England a few years later, in 1660.

Origins of the Stone

Scone was the capital of the Pictish kingdom and was the seat of Kenneth MacAlpin, who united Scotland, from AD 843. The stone, a piece of red sandstone over 400 million years old, was possibly already in place and could have formed an important part of a pagan ceremony. Geological studies have shown it to be virtually identical to other rocks in the Scone area.

The Stone was seen as a symbol of Scotland's nationhood and its significance was to increase after it was stolen by Edward I in 1296. Edward had taken the Stone as a war trophy, determined to exert his authority and crush the independence of the Scots. He had it removed and taken to Westminster Abbey, where in 1297 it was installed beneath the Coronation Chair. Some have claimed that Edward was palmed off with a fake – perhaps even a drainage cover. However this is unlikely, as his officials had already seen the Stone, which has a smooth surface and some distinctive markings.

Origins of the Stone

The Scots appealed to the Pope to help them get the Stone returned and, because it apparently had no intrinsic value or aesthetic appeal, the lawyer arguing their case embellished his story of how important it was by claiming that the Stone had been brought to Scotland from Egypt by a pharaoh's daughter. Further myths began to spring up and some even claimed that the Stone was Jacob's pillow.

The Stone continued to play its role in history, as all English monarchs from 1297 were crowned upon it. It also continued to be seen as a symbol of Scottish independence and many resented its presence in London. In 1950 some Scottish students managed to steal it from Westminster Abbey, but it was retrieved and replaced. However, in 1996 the Stone was returned to the Scots. It was escorted with due ceremony and put on display in Edinburgh Castle. Many hope that one day it will return to Scone.

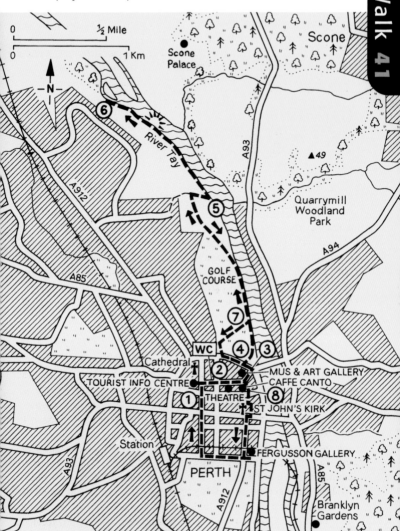

Walk 41 **Directions**

① From the tourist information centre turn right, then take the first right so that you walk round the building. Turn right again and walk down to reach the road. Cross over and take the right-hand road ahead, passing the bus stops. Walk down to reach **Kinnoul Street**, then cross over and join **Mill Street**.

Walk 41

② Continue down Mill Street, passing **Perth Theatre** on the right-hand side. Keep walking ahead, pass **Caffe Canto** (➤ Where to Eat and Drink) on the right-hand side, and join **Bridge Lane**. You'll pass the museum and art gallery on the left-hand side and will come on to **Charlotte Street**. Turn left here.

WHAT TO LOOK FOR ℹ

St John's Kirk, which you pass on this walk, was founded in 1126 – though most of the present building dates from the 15th century. It gave the town its original name 'St John's town' – now the name of the local football team, St Johnstone. John Knox gave a sermon here that inspired local people to sack the nearby monasteries.

---

③ At the corner you can turn left if you wish to visit the **Fair Maid's House**. Otherwise, cross over the road and turn right through the park. Walk past the **war memorial** then bear left to join the riverside path. This will give you good views of the smart houses along the opposite bank.

④ Continue ahead on the path, passing the golf course. When you reach the sign for the 14th tee, turn right and follow the track. At the end there's a wall on the left. You can choose to go either to the left of the wall along an enclosed cycle track (keeping an ear open for cyclists), or to the right of it to walk by the water's edge.

WHERE TO EAT AND DRINK ℹ

Caffe Canto on George Street is a chic café and a good spot to enjoy a creamy cappuccino and a cake or a light lunch such as a panini. Pubs worth trying include the **Auld Hoose**, **Mucky Mulligan's** or the **Cherrybank**. All serve bar meals.

---

⑤ Follow your chosen track until the two tracks meet, just past an electricity sub station. Walk by the riverside now to enjoy great views of Scone Palace on the opposite bank – there's a seat so you can sneak a rest. This is a lovely spot on a warm, summer's day.

⑥ Retrace your steps now, walking back beside the river or along the cycle track and back to the **golf course**. Turn left and walk back towards Perth until you reach the cricket and football pitches on the right-hand side.

⑦ Turn right and walk between the pitches to join **Rose Terrace** – John Ruskin once lived here. Turn left, then bear left at the end into **Charlotte Street** and right into **Bridge Lane** again. Turn left along **Skinner Gate**, the site of the oldest pub in Perth, and walk along to the end.

WHILE YOU'RE THERE ℹ

If you like gardens, make for **Branklyn Gardens** on Dundee Road. This 2 acre (0.8ha) private garden contains lots of unusual and rare plants, including gorgeous Himalayan poppies – they're the bright blue ones. There are more plants at **Bell's Cherrybank Centre**, the home of Bell's Scotch Whisky and the National Heather Collection. There are over 900 varieties of heather on display.

---

⑧ Cross over to pass **St John's Kirk** (➤ What to Look For). Cross **South Street** and join **Princes Street**. At **Marshall Place** turn left and walk to the **Fergusson Gallery** on the left-hand side. Then turn back along **Marshall Place**, walk up to **King Street**, then turn right. Maintain direction now, then turn left into **West Mill Street** and return to the start of the walk.

An Ancient Yew in Fortingall

Discover the history of an extraordinary tree on this easy walk amidst stunning mountain scenery.

•DISTANCE•	4½ miles (7.2km)
•MINIMUM TIME•	2hrs
•ASCENT / GRADIENT•	33ft (10m) ▲▲▲
•LEVEL OF DIFFICULTY•	林林 林林 林林
•PATHS•	Quiet roads and firm farm tracks, 1 stile
•LANDSCAPE•	Picture postcard Scottish scenery, ancient tree
•SUGGESTED MAP•	aqua3 OS Explorer 378 Ben Lawers & Glen Lyon
•START / FINISH•	Grid reference: NN 741470
•DOG FRIENDLINESS•	Best to keep them on lead in case of cars
•PARKING•	Fortingall village
•PUBLIC TOILETS•	None on route; nearest in Aberfeldy

BACKGROUND TO THE WALK

Take a good look at the yew tree in the churchyard at the start of this walk. It is the oldest living thing in Europe – possibly even the world. No one knows exactly how old it is, as yews are notoriously difficult to date (their heartwood dies and they become hollow after around 500 years). However, it is generally reckoned to be around 5,000 years old. Some people think it could even be older – up to 9,000 years. In 1769 the tree's girth was measured and found to be 56ft (17m).

A Special Tree

Long before Christianity, yew trees were held sacred by the Druids and the Celts. This must surely be because of the tree's extraordinary powers of regeneration; they can enter long periods of 'hibernation' when they hardly grow at all – and then suddenly sprout new leaves. Some think yews were planted over graves so as to protect and purify the dead – others think that sacred sites and burial grounds grew up beside already existing yew trees. What is certain is that they have a special place in our culture. Like many other pagan symbols, the significance of yew trees was retained and sanctified by the early Christian Church and you will frequently see yew trees in churchyards today. There are at least 500 churchyards in England and Wales that have yews as old as the church itself, and many of the trees are much older than the building.

Rock a Bye Baby

During medieval times, yews were often placed in churchyards alongside the route that coffins would take. Some think trees were also planted here to provide wood for longbows, while keeping their poisonous branches out of the reach of cattle. The branches of yew trees were also used as church decoration. One famous yew tree in Derbyshire is said to have provided the inspiration for the nursery rhyme *Rock a Bye Baby*. It's known as the Betty Kenny tree and was once the home of a local family. A child's cradle was created in one of

Walk 42

the boughs. Yew trees were also sometimes planted beside inns as a sign to travellers. Two yews were said to indicate that accommodation was available. Three yews meant that the inn was able to make provision for the travellers' animals as well.

Pilate Was Here?

Fortingall is also said to have been the birthplace of Pontius Pilate, who is reputed to have played under the branches of the tree. Apparently Pilate's father was an officer in the Roman army and was stationed here with his wife during the Roman occupation. The family was said to have left Scotland when Pilate was young. However, some claim that Pilate eventually returned to Fortingall and is buried in the churchyard.

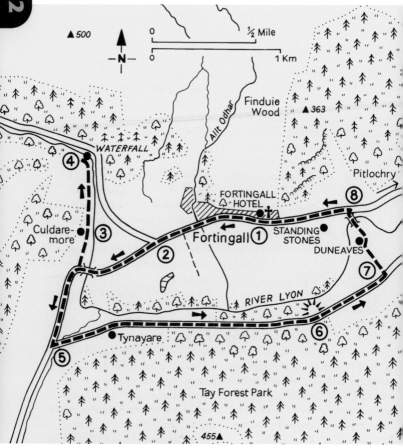

Walk 42 Directions

① With your back to the **Fortingall Hotel**, turn right along the road, passing several pretty thatched cottages (an unusual sight in Scotland) on the right-hand side.

Follow the road over a burn and then past the entrance to **Glen Lyon farm**. Eventually you'll reach a fork in the road.

② Ignore the right-hand fork and maintain direction. The road will soon take you over a bridge that

Walk 42

crosses the **River Lyon**. Just over the bridge turn right to follow a track. You'll soon pass a large, attractive house on the left-hand side and will go through two gates.

③ Maintain your direction and walk round the field edge with the river below you on the right-hand side. You'll soon spy a stile in the fence on the right. Nip over this and you'll come to a secret spot under the trees by **Sput Ban** waterfall – it's a lovely place for a picnic.

④ Hop back over the stile and retrace your steps past the house and back to the road. Turn right and follow the road (it's tarmacked but very quiet), and walk past some little cottages on the right-hand side. Continue until you reach the sign for Duneaves.

⑤ Turn left and follow the road – the river is on your left-hand side. You feel as if you're in a secret valley as you walk along here, and in late summer you can stop to pick the wild raspberries that grow by the roadside. Continue past an area of woodland, after which you get views across the valley to Fortingall.

⑥ Continue to follow the road until you see a white house on the right-hand side. Leave the metalled track and turn left at the pylon just before the house – the views of the surrounding hills are great.

⑦ Follow the wide, stony track as it leads down to **Duneaves**. Just before you reach the house go through the rusty gate in the wall on the right-hand side. Then walk across the field, maintaining your direction to go over a rather bouncy footbridge. Bear right after crossing the bridge, then go through the gate and join the road.

⑧ Turn left and walk back along the road. You'll soon pass two sets of standing stones in the field on the left – six stones in a ring near the road, and three further away. Walk back into **Fortingall** to reach your starting place.

The Sweet Fruits of Alyth

This varied walk takes you through the fertile heart of Scotland.

Walk 43

•DISTANCE•	5 miles (8km)
•MINIMUM TIME•	3hrs
•ASCENT / GRADIENT•	787ft (240m) ▲▲ ▲▲ ▲
•LEVEL OF DIFFICULTY•	🚶🚶 🚶🚶 🚶🚶
•PATHS•	Wide grassy tracks, some rougher paths on hill
•LANDSCAPE•	Mixed woodland, overgrown pasture and gentle hills
•SUGGESTED MAP•	aqua3 OS Explorer 381 Blairgowrie, Kirriemuir & Glamis
•START / FINISH•	Grid reference: NO 236486
•DOG FRIENDLINESS•	Can run free in many places – keep on lead near sheep
•PARKING•	Car park in Alyth Market Square
•PUBLIC TOILETS•	Near Alyth Market Square

BACKGROUND TO THE WALK

If you do this walk in the summer or early autumn, put some plastic bowls in the car before you go. That's because Alyth is close to Blairgowrie, and is surrounded by the soft fruit fields of Strathmore. Although you don't pass any strawberry fields on the walk, there are many just a short drive away and you'll see 'Pick your own' signs everywhere.

Fabulous Fruits

This part of Scotland has long been famed for the quality of its soft fruit, particularly its strawberries and raspberries. The land is fertile and the climate mild – perfect for raising sweet, juicy berries. You will see many fields covered in a layer of fine fleece, placed there to protect the strawberry plants, particularly from birds. Fruits from the fields used to be picked to serve the jam-making industry of nearby Dundee. The area's importance for fruit growing is reflected in the names of many varieties of berry. There's the Tayberry (a cross between a blackberry and a raspberry), which refers to the nearby Tay, as well as varieties of raspberry such as Glen Clova and Glen Prosen (both glens being just a short distance from Alyth).

These soft fruits have played an important part in the British diet for a long time, providing valuable vitamin C. Wild strawberries and raspberries are both native to Britain. Strawberries were cultivated in Elizabethan times, although the cultivated ones you buy today are more likely to come from non-native stock: a Chilean species, for example, was introduced in the 1800s and produced larger, more brightly coloured fruits.

Today we tend to use soft fruits for jam or simply eat them fresh, often with lashings of cream. However, they were once used in much more complicated recipes. An Elizabethan book, first printed in 1596 and entitled *The Good Huswifes Jewell*, describes a recipe for Tarte of Strawberries that begins: 'Take strawberries and washe them in claret wine, thicke and temper them with rose-water, and season them with cinamon, sugar, and ginger…' Sounds pretty good actually.

Not only were soft fruits eaten, they were once used to make medicines. Culpeper, the famous 17th-century physician and herbalist, described the versatile healing properties of strawberries in some detail, declaring that the plants were ruled by the planet Venus and

Walk 43

that the berries were 'excellent good to cool the liver, the blood, and the spleen, or an hot choleric stomach.' He declared that lotions made from the leaves and roots of strawberries could help ulcers in the 'privy parts' and were also good 'to fasten loose teeth, and to heal spungy foul gums.' Even today, raspberry leaf tea is drunk by women to help them in the final stages of pregnancy and during labour, while raspberry vinegar makes an excellent gargle for soothing sore throats.

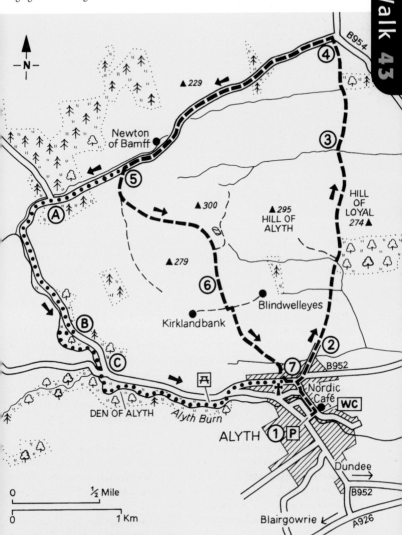

Walk 43 **Directions**

① From the **Market Square**, cross the burn, then turn left along **Commercial Street**, so that the river is on your left-hand side. Turn right up **Tootie Street**, right again up **Hill Street**, then take **Loyal Road** on the left. Continue walking uphill to reach a sign for 'Hill of Loyal Walk'.

Walk 43

② Walk uphill now, go through a gate and continue in the same direction, walking past a wood on the right-hand side. You'll go through a kissing gate, passing an area that in summer is a mass of purple foxgloves. Eventually your path levels out and then starts to bear downhill. Maintain your direction to go through a kissing gate and over a burn.

WHERE TO EAT AND DRINK
The **Nordic Café** is on Mill Street, by the Market Square in Alyth. It's clean and contemporary inside, and the owner is friendly to walkers. The food served ranges from baked potatoes and toasties to open sandwiches, ice creams and cappuccinos. It also operates as a little art gallery and many works are for sale.

③ From this point the path becomes narrower and bears uphill again, becoming muddier and more overgrown. You'll walk under trees now, through a gate, and will then leave the birch and oak woodland. Keep an eye out for deer here, as I spotted one bounding into the trees, just a few feet away from me. Maintain your direction through the grass, then go through a kissing gate to reach the road.

④ Turn left and walk along the road, following the signs to the Hill of Alyth Walk. It's pretty quiet along here, so you should meet few cars. The road takes you past a conifer plantation, past a house on the right-hand side and over a cattle grid. Soon after this, you turn left and follow the signs for the Cateran Trail.

⑤ Walk uphill and, at a crossing of tracks, turn to the right. When the ground flattens, turn left uphill. When you reach another crossing

WHILE YOU'RE THERE
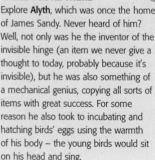
Explore **Alyth**, which was once the home of James Sandy. Never heard of him? Well, not only was he the inventor of the invisible hinge (an item we never give a thought to today, probably because it's invisible), but he was also something of a mechanical genius, copying all sorts of items with great success. For some reason he also took to incubating and hatching birds' eggs using the warmth of his body – the young birds would sit on his head and sing.

of paths, turn right. There are lots of paths traversing the hill, so you can choose your own route at this point, but essentially you must keep the lakes on your left and don't walk as far as the beacon. Make for a small copse on your right, between two farmhouses, then go through a gate.

⑥ Walk downhill along the enclosed track – you'll see the spire of the church below you. When you reach another track turn left, then right to continue walking downhill on a metalled track. Walk under a line of pylons and come into the village by the church.

⑦ Your path now bears left and takes you downhill, past a phone box on the left-hand side. Turn right, walking past the crumbling old arches, and retrace your steps to the start of the walk in the **Market Square**.

WHAT TO LOOK FOR

Do this walk in summer and you will see many **foxgloves**. These distinctive plants are native to Britain and love to grow in open places. They are extremely poisonous, but also have a medical use: digitalis, a powerful drug, is prepared from the leaves and used to treat heart disease.

Walk 44

And Through the Den of Alyth

A longer walk by a pretty burn.
See map and information panel for Walk 43

•DISTANCE•	6½ miles (10.4km)
•MINIMUM TIME•	4hrs
•ASCENT / GRADIENT•	558ft (170m) ▲ ▲ ▲
•LEVEL OF DIFFICULTY•	🚶🚶 🚶🚶 🚶🚶

Walk 44 Directions (Walk 43 option)

At Point ⑤ on the main route, continue following the road – there are pleasant views on your right-hand side as the ground drops away steeply. Cross a cattle grid and continue ahead with conifers on either side.

The road now winds downhill and brings you to a junction (Point Ⓐ). Turn left here – it's signed 'Alyth 2' – and continue following the road as it bends through the trees. Keep on this road until you reach a path that drops steeply down to the right through the trees (Point Ⓑ).

When you reach the bottom, go to the left and follow the path that runs by the river. This area is known as the **Den of Alyth** and is a Site of Special Scientific Interest (SSSI). The area has been wooded for thousands of years and is a mixed wood, with beech, alder, oak, ash and hazel trees.

When you come to a house on the right-hand side, maintain direction to go down steps and continue walking beside the river (Point Ⓒ). Follow the path and you'll eventually come to a picnic/play area on the left-hand side. Continue to walk beside the river until you join the main road. Turn right here and walk along the road to reach the centre of **Alyth** again.

WHILE YOU'RE THERE

It's worth driving into **Dundee**, the city on the Tay that is famed in Scotland for the three J's: Jam, Jute and Journalism. The jam industry was supported by the soft fruits grown in the fields around Alyth and nearby Blairgowrie. It was a highly successful industry but began almost by accident. A ship carrying a cargo of oranges took refuge in Dundee harbour during a storm. The fruit could have gone to waste, but an enterprising local grocer bought it and his wife made the oranges into marmalade. Jute, which is made from strong plant fibres, was traded in Dundee from the 19th century and was used to make sacks as well as items such as stage wigs and hair pieces. Dundee's other 'J' – journalism – refers to the presence of the publishers D C Thomson, who still produce newspapers and magazines. Dundee was also an important ship-building centre and the home of the *Discovery*, Captain Scott's ship which was launched here in 1901. The ship is moored here today and has a good visitor centre and on-board displays.

Walk 45

Macbeth's Battle at Kinrossie

An easy walk to the site of Macbeth's famous defeat.

·DISTANCE·	5 miles (8km)
·MINIMUM TIME·	1hr 40min
·ASCENT / GRADIENT·	591ft (180m) ▲▲▲
·LEVEL OF DIFFICULTY·	🚶🚶 🚶🚶 🚶🚶
·PATHS·	Quiet roads, one grassy hill track
·LANDSCAPE·	Quiet villages, fields and historic hills
·SUGGESTED MAP·	aqua3 OS Explorer 380 Dundee & Sidlaw Hills
·START / FINISH·	Grid reference: NO 188323
·DOG FRIENDLINESS·	No dogs on Dunsinane Hill
·PARKING·	Kinrossie main street
·PUBLIC TOILETS·	None on route

Walk 45 Directions

'Macbeth shall never
vanquish'd be until
Great Birnam wood to high
Dunsinane hill
Shall come against him'
    from *Macbeth*,
    William Shakespeare

Well, we all know what happened – in the play, at least. Although Shakespeare's version of Macbeth's life is far from the truth and builds on legends that grew up after his death, there certainly was a battle on Dunsinane (or Dunsinnan) Hill in Perthshire, which is topped with an ancient earthwork. This easy walk takes you to this historic site and gives you the chance to discover the real Macbeth.

From the old cross by the thatched cottage on the main street, walk through the village, keeping the cross on your left-hand side. At the end of the street, turn right along the road signposted 'Collace Church and School'. This is a very quiet road with mature trees on either side. Walk up until you reach **Collace church**. Just in front of the church, turn right and follow the obvious track. Follow it past a farm on your left, and continue following it as it narrows. It does get very overgrown in the middle, but just keep walking in the same direction. Eventually the path opens out and you'll come to a road. Turn left and walk down to the junction, then turn left again to follow the road. You'll eventually pass a patch of woodland on your right-hand side and will then come to some houses on the left – behind which is the site of an ancient stone circle.

Early sources state that Macbeth was a popular King, 'fair, yellow-haired and tall', who reigned from AD 1040 to 1057. His name

---

WHILE YOU'RE THERE ⓘ

The **Meikleour Beech Hedge** is a short drive from Kinrossie, on the A93 east of Dunkeld. It's a living wall of glorious beech trees stretching 100 ft (30m) high and ½mile (530m) long. Planted in 1745, it is the highest hedge in the world.

Walk 45

WHERE TO EAT AND DRINK ⓘ

There's nowhere in Kinrossie but further down the road at Balbeggie is the **MacDonald Arms**. They've got an extensive menu, and serve bar meals like baked potatoes, fish and chips and toasties, as well as offering more substantial dishes in their restaurant. There are plenty of veggie choices, too.

MacBeathadh means 'son of life' and he was the son of Findlaech mac Ruaidri, who was the Mormaer (or great steward) of Moray – a title which had the status of an English earl. Macbeth was born at a time when the Scottish succession was flexible and traditionally alternated between relatives and certain clans. The system of primogeniture practised in England did not exist and, when a king died, the throne was essentially 'up for grabs'. Macbeth belonged to a clan that had a claim to the throne. In 1020 Findlaech was murdered by three of his nephews, one of whom was later burned to death. Many think Macbeth was involved in this, particularly as he then married the dead man's widow Gruoch (the real Lady Macbeth), who had a strong royal pedigree. The marriage certainly strengthened Macbeth's claim to the throne. Macbeth became war leader to the young Scottish King Duncan, who reigned for only a few years before he was murdered 'by his own people'. Macbeth has been blamed for his death, too, by one authority. There is little evidence for this, but the murder was certainly to his advantage, for he succeeded Duncan as King in 1040.

Walk past the pine woods on the left-hand side until you reach a junction. Turn left here – it's signed 'Collace' – and follow the road. It's a pretty quiet road but do keep an eye out for traffic. You'll pass woods on the left that encircle a hill known as **Bandirran Hill**. Walk past the quarry on your right-hand side and continue following the road until you reach a gate on the right-hand side. Go through the kissing gate next to the gate (there's a sign saying 'No dogs – Beware of bull') and walk up the grassy track, keeping the fence line on the left-hand side. You'll eventually pass a patch of wood and then leave the fence line to continue uphill. At the top you come to the ancient fortifications on **Dunsinane Hill**.

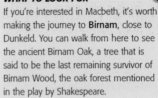

WHAT TO LOOK FOR ⓘ

If you're interested in Macbeth, it's worth making the journey to **Birnam**, close to Dunkeld. You can walk from here to see the ancient Birnam Oak, a tree that is said to be the last remaining survivor of Birnam Wood, the oak forest mentioned in the play by Shakespeare.

While Macbeth, now King, undertook a pilgrimage to Rome, Duncan's son, Malcolm Canmore, was making plans to avenge his father's death and regain the throne of Scotland. In 1054 he and his troops marched against Macbeth and fought a battle on Dunsinane Hill. Macbeth was defeated and fled to Aberdeenshire, where a few years later he was killed by Malcolm in a final battle.

Now retrace your steps to re-join the road and turn right to walk through **Collace** village. After the village, keep following the road to reach a junction. Turn left and walk along the narrow road to reach the church again. Turn right, in front of the church, and walk back along the road. At the end, turn left to return to the starting point in **Kinrossie**.

Walk 46

Antarctic Dreams in Glen Prosen

From the most peaceful of the Angus Glens, walk across hills once trodden by Captain Scott.

•DISTANCE•	4 miles (6.4km)
•MINIMUM TIME•	1hr 50min
•ASCENT / GRADIENT•	620ft (190m) ▲ ▲ ▲
•LEVEL OF DIFFICULTY•	🚶 🚶 🚶
•PATHS•	Wide firm moorland and woodland tracks, one quiet road
•LANDSCAPE•	Remote hills, moors and historic valley
•SUGGESTED MAP•	aqua3 OS Explorer 388 Lochnagar, Glen Muick
•START / FINISH•	Grid reference: NO 328657
•DOG FRIENDLINESS•	Good, can run free for much of way
•PARKING•	By Glen Prosen church
•PUBLIC TOILETS•	None on route

BACKGROUND TO THE WALK

There is something immensely peaceful about Glen Prosen. That's partly because it is one of the least known of the Angus Glens – many Scots haven't even heard of it. But it also has a tranquil, almost magical atmosphere. However, this lovely place has links to an historic and ultimately tragic journey – for it was in a cottage here that Captain Scott, together with Edward Wilson, planned and prepared for their ill-fated journey to the South Pole.

A cairn at the top of the glen commemorates this sad association, bearing the inscription: 'For the journey is done and the summit attained and the barriers fall.'

Scott had joined the navy in 1881 and, from 1900 to 1904, commanded the National Antarctic Expedition in the *Discovery*, the first specially designed scientific research ship, built in nearby Dundee. The ship withstood two winters in the Antarctic and Scott and his team explored the Ross Sea and discovered King Edward VII Land.

Pipped at the Post

A few years later, in 1910, Scott, together with Wilson, Laurence Oates, Edward Evans and Henry Bowers, set off on another polar journey. They sailed in another Dundee-built vessel, the *Terra Nova*, with the aim of becoming the first men to reach the South Pole. They marched and skied over 900 miles (1,458km) of frozen wastes, living largely on hard tack biscuits and 'pemmican', a mix of lard and dried beef. They eventually reached the Pole on 17 January 1912, only to discover that a Norwegian expedition led by Roald Amundsen had beaten them by a month.

Unfortunately on the return journey they were delayed by blizzards and the illness of Evans, who died. The conditions they had to endure were appalling and Oates got severe frostbite in his feet, which made him lame and slowed the party down considerably. Concerned that he was becoming a burden to his companions, Oates heroically sacrificed himself by walking out of the tent into a blizzard, saying: 'I'm just going outside and may be some time.'

Walk 46

Journey's End

However, Oates' brave action was not enough to save the other members of the expedition. Although they continued their journey, they were eventually beaten by the severe weather and died in March. Their bodies were found by a search party eight months later, together with their diaries.

Captain Scott's efforts did not go unrecognised or unrewarded. He was posthumously knighted and a polar research institute was established in his memory. One of his last letters from the ice cap was written to his friend J M Barrie, who was born and brought up at Kirriemuir, just a few miles from Glen Prosen. In anticipation of his impending death, Scott asked Barrie to help his widow and son and said: 'I can never show you how much your friendship meant to me.'

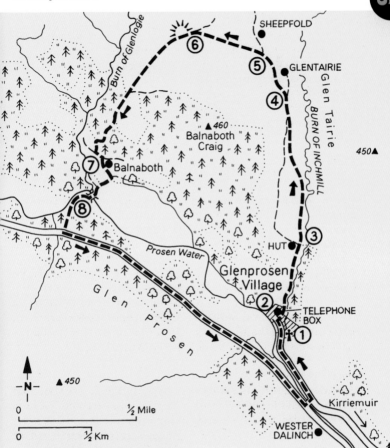

Walk 46 Directions

① From the church in **Glenprosen Village**, walk on to the road and turn right to cross the little bridge. Walk past **Burnmouth Cottage** on the right-hand side, then turn right in front of the telephone box. Walk uphill and join the wide gravel track ahead.

② Follow the track as it takes you past a wood on the right-hand side

Walk 46

– you'll hear the water of the Burn of Inchmill below. Continue along this obvious track to reach some caravans and a small hut on the left.

③ Go through the gate on the right and maintain direction as the track takes you past bare, heather-clad hills. You'll pass conifer forest on the left and will soon see **Glentairie house** ahead. Shortly before you reach the house, look for an old fence post on the right and the remains of a wall on the left. Bear left here.

WHERE TO EAT AND DRINK ℹ
Visocchi's in Kirriemuir is a bustling ice cream parlour dating back to the 1930s. As well as delicious sundaes and ices, it serves hot drinks, baked potatoes and toasties. It has plenty of atmosphere, with old photographs and original price lists from the 1930s displayed on the walls. In those days, a plain ice, a hot Bovril or a cup of cocoa was 4*d*, while a Kola (sic) was 3*d*.

④ Follow the track as it swings past the house. Keep the house on your right, then join the fence line on the right-hand side. Walk up to reach a shallow gully, with an old **sheepfold** ahead of you.

⑤ Turn left, leaving the sheepfold behind and keeping the gully to your right. Maintain direction now, with the conifer plantation on your left, and keep going to reach a fence. Go through the gate and enjoy the views over the valley below.

⑥ Follow the track swinging left, bouncing downhill between thick clumps of heather. At the bottom, go through the metal gate and walk through the forest. After going through another gate, turn right on to the wide track. At a crossing of

WHILE YOU'RE THERE ℹ
Kirriemuir was the birthplace of J M Barrie, the author of *Peter Pan and the Lost Boys* (1904). He was the son of a local weaver and you can visit his home, which is now a museum. One of Barrie's older brothers died when he was a child, and he was said to have been greatly affected by his death. It was said to have inspired the play *Peter Pan*, about the boy who never grew up.

tracks turn left, bearing downhill. Pass a couple of footbridges and three cottages, to reach a large house with a wide lawn.

⑦ Walk in front of the house, pass another footbridge, then leave the tarmac track to join the grassy track by the river. Pass yet another footbridge at the junction of the rivers and cross the second footbridge that takes you over the larger river.

⑧ Turn right along the obvious track, go through a metal gate, and walk uphill to join the road. Turn left now and walk along the road until you reach the turning on the left just before **Wester Dalinch farm** – signed 'Prosen Village'. Turn left here, cross the bridge, then go left on the other side to return to **Glenprosen Village**.

WHAT TO LOOK FOR ℹ
You will see plenty of **lichens** on this walk, particularly on the last section where they hang from the branches of mature birch trees. Lichens are very sensitive to pollution and don't grow in places where the air is contaminated. This makes them a useful 'indicator species', meaning that their presence or absence tells you something about the environment. The healthy lichens here are a sign that the air is particularly clear and clean.

The Inspirational Landscape of Auchenblae

Walk through the fields and woods of the Howe of Mearns, which inspired a Scottish writer.

·DISTANCE·	4½ miles (7.2km)
·MINIMUM TIME·	2hrs 20min
·ASCENT / GRADIENT·	459ft (140m) ▲▲▲
·LEVEL OF DIFFICULTY·	🚶 🚶 🚶
·PATHS·	Established footpaths, overgrown woodland tracks
·LANDSCAPE·	Acres of arable fields and cool forests
·SUGGESTED MAP·	aqua3 OS Explorer 396 Stonehaven, Inverbervie & Lawrencekirk
·START / FINISH·	Grid reference: NO 727787
·DOG FRIENDLINESS·	Fallen trees make it unsuitable except for fit dogs
·PARKING·	On street in Auchenblae
·PUBLIC TOILETS·	Off main street in Auchenblae

BACKGROUND TO THE WALK

> '…you'd waken with the peewits crying across the hills, deep and deep, crying in the heart of you … almost you'd cry for that, the beauty of it and the sweetness of the Scottish land and skies'
>
> *Sunset Song*, 1932

Those words were written by James Leslie Mitchell and seem to sum up the immense love and affection he had for his native Howe of the Mearns in north east Scotland. It is fertile land, south of Aberdeen. This walk introduces you to this little-walked part of the country, an area that will forever be associated with the author.

Mitchell is better known by his pen name of Lewis Grassic Gibbon. He was born in 1901 into a crofting family and had no illusions about the toughness of life on the land. He once wrote: 'My mother used to hap me in a plaid in harvest time and leave me in the lea of a stook while she harvested.' In his books he portrayed the breakdown of crofting life, but did not gloss over its hardships.

Crofter to Author

Gibbon became a journalist at the age of 16 and joined the *Aberdeen Journal*, and later the *Scottish Farmer* in Glasgow. He became ill and moved back home to work in the fields before joining the army as a clerk, later moving into the RAF. He travelled to Central America to see the remains of the Maya civilization, and later claimed that his digestion was forever affected by the enforced local diet of maize.

Gibbon left the forces in 1929 and returned to Britain, living in the south of England and trying to make his name as a writer. His first book was *Sunset Song*, set in the Howe of the Mearns and telling the tale of Chris Guthrie, who was torn between her desire to escape her small community and her love for the land. He wrote it in six weeks. It was the first of a trilogy, known as *A Scots Quair* (or 'quire' – a volume) and was rapidly followed by the other books *Cloud Howe* (1933) and *Grey Granite* (1934).

A Short but Prolific Life

Gibbon was extremely disciplined and driven – it was as if he knew he did not have much time to make his name. He divided each day into three and aimed to write 1,500 words in each session. He made some mistakes at first and tried to sell some of his short stories to the wrong type of magazines. However, H G Wells took an interest in his work and suggested different publications for him to try. Lewis Grassic Gibbon eventually died in 1935 of a duodenal ulcer. He was just 34 and had written 16 books.

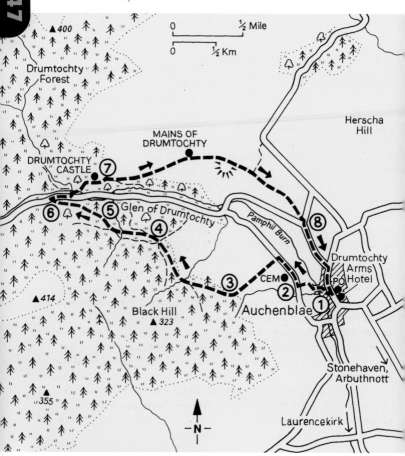

Walk 47 **Directions**

① With your back to the **post office** on the main street, turn right and cross over to follow the signs that say 'Woodland Walk'. Go down the tarmac slope, past a play area,

then go over a bridge. Follow this track uphill, passing woodland on your right, and continue until you reach a road.

② Turn right and walk along this long, straight road, passing a cemetery. You then take the first

Walk **47**

turning on the left, which runs between arable fields. Continue walking to reach the wood ahead. You'll now have to shift a rusty gate and scramble through some undergrowth to get into the woods and join a track.

WHERE TO EAT AND DRINK ⓘ

The **Drumtochty Arms Hotel** is a little pub in the village where you can get a drink if you're thirsty. Otherwise try the little village of Inverbervie on the coast, where there are a few places to choose from. There's a well-known fish and chip shop there called the **Bervie Chipper**, which has won awards for its food.

---

③ Turn right and follow the track round the margin of the woods – it is thickly carpeted with vegetation. When you reach a wider gravel track, turn right and continue – fields will still be visible through the trees on the right-hand side. Follow this track until you reach a crossing of tracks.

④ Take the left-hand fork now. When you reach a pylon on the right-hand side of the track, strike off on the indistinct track that runs downhill to the right under the line of pylons. (If you go under the pylons on the main track, you've gone too far.)

⑤ Scramble through the undergrowth now and follow the indistinct track as it swings round to the left, bearing in a north westerly direction. When I was last here I had to negotiate my way past a number of fallen trees at this point, which had been damaged by a recent storm – so do be careful, as some of them were pretty large. Eventually you will come down to meet the main road.

⑥ Turn right and follow the road, then turn left through the white gates to **Drumtochty Castle** – marked 'Private Residence'. Pass a house, cross a burn by a car park, then bear right at the meeting of three tracks, following the middle track, past a pool and a lake. Walk past Drumtochty Castle and swing up to the gates.

⑦ Follow the track that bears to the right, leaving the castle behind you. At a fork, bear left and continue along an avenue of beech trees. Pass the farmhouse, **Mains of Drumtochty**, then maintain your direction, following the track which has great views over the Howe of the Mearns. Continue ahead to go under a line of pylons and meet the road.

⑧ Turn right along the road for a few paces, then go left at the junction and follow the road back into **Auchenblae**. When you reach the main street, turn right and walk back to the starting point of the walk.

WHILE YOU'RE THERE ⓘ

The **Lewis Grassic Gibbon Centre** is in the village of Arbuthnott, which has strong associations with the author. The centre has displays telling the story of his short but productive life and gives an introduction to the area that inspired his work. In the churchyard you can see the grave marking the place were his ashes were buried. Other places to explore in the Howe of the Mearns include the pretty town of **Laurencekirk**, close to which is the Hill of Garvock from which you get great views over the land. You can also go to **Fettercairn**. Among its attractions is the nearby distillery. It's one of the oldest in Scotland.

The Mysterious Stones of Aberlemno

This walk takes you through agricultural land once inhabited by the Picts, a fascinating ancient British tribe.

•DISTANCE•	3 miles (4.8km)
•MINIMUM TIME•	1hr 45min
•ASCENT / GRADIENT•	394ft (120m) ▲▲ ▲▲ ▲
•LEVEL OF DIFFICULTY•	🚶🚶 🚶🚶 🚶
•PATHS•	Mainly quiet roads but one extremely overgrown area
•LANDSCAPE•	Quiet agricultural land and ancient carved stones
•SUGGESTED MAP•	aqua3 OS Explorer 389 Forfar, Brechin & Edzell
•START / FINISH•	Grid reference: NO 522558
•DOG FRIENDLINESS•	Overgrown area makes this unsuitable for dogs
•PARKING•	Car park by school in Aberlemno
•PUBLIC TOILETS•	None on route; nearest in Forfar

BACKGROUND TO THE WALK

Had history turned out differently, you would have been doing this walk in Pictland, not Scotland. The Picts inhabited this northern part of Britain for thousands of years, yet today we know little about them. Neither their language nor any of their manuscripts have survived and their culture is something of a mystery. The best reminders we have of them are the intriguing carved stones that dot the landscape of eastern Scotland – the greatest concentration being in Angus and around the Moray Firth. You can see several of these beautiful pieces of ancient art on this walk, which takes you through the heart of the land of the Picts.

The Painted Ones

Mystery surrounds the origins of the Picts. The only thing that seems to be certain is that they occupied what we now call Scotland when the Romans arrived and they may have been here for over 1,000 years before that. The Roman Empire soon stretched from southern England to the central belt of Scotland, and the culture and language of the tribes living under the occupation gradually began to alter under their influence. However, the Romans never spread north of the Forth–Clyde line, and so the tribes there kept their distinct language and customs. The Romans called them the Picti, Latin for 'painted ones' – a reference to their warriors' continued habit of daubing themselves in woad.

After the fall of the Roman Empire, new tribes began to invade Britain, with the Angles and Saxons gradually conquering the south, and Gaelic speakers from Ireland, who called themselves Scotti – or Scots – moving into the far north west. Perhaps to assert their identity, the Picts began to carve detailed symbols on to stones, possibly using them to delineate territory held by different tribal chiefs.

The Picts were pagan, but had been exposed to Christian ideas from around AD 400, brought to their country by the Celtic missionary Ninian, and later by Columba. In AD 565 Columba travelled to Inverness to meet a powerful Pictish king, Bridei. They had a competition to see whether Columba's miracles could beat Pictish magic. It isn't clear who won, but gradually the Picts converted to Christianity.

The End of an Era

Of course there were wars between the various tribes, the Picts fighting the Gaels and Angles, as well as battling among themselves. The carved stone that you pass in Aberlemno churchyard is thought to commemorate one of Bridei's major victories. Stone carving became more and more important in their culture, with increasingly intricate patterns being created, often combined with a Christian cross. However, in AD 794 the Vikings began to raid northern and western Scotland, weakening the Pictish kingdom. The Gaelic-speaking Scots saw their opportunity – in 843 a Scot called Kenneth MacAlpin seized their throne, and the Pictish nation died.

Walk 48 **Directions**

① From the car park turn right and walk along the road, then go first left, signed 'Aberlemno church and stone'. Walk past the church – the famous **Pictish stone** is in the churchyard – and follow the road as it bends round to the right. Follow the road until you reach a T-junction.

② Turn right and follow this road, passing the entrance to **Woodside** on the left. At the corner, follow the road as it bends right. Walk down to join the **B9134**, turn right and follow this a short distance until you reach a turning on the left.

③ Turn left along this road, signed 'Finavon Hill', passing a house at the bottom called **Hillcrest**. The road winds uphill, past several rocky outcrops, then under a line of pylons. Continue on this road as it skirts a hill, with areas of new tree planting on the left.

WHAT TO LOOK FOR ⓘ

Take a good look at the **carvings** on the Aberlemno stones. No one truly understands the symbols carved on Pictish stones, but they seem to represent a special writing system. Stones are carved with scenes of warriors and battles; with spirals and complex patterns; with simple geometrical shapes; with wild creatures such as stags, wolves and eagles; and even with everyday objects, like combs.

---

④ Continue following the road and you will soon see a mast, followed by a pond on the left, and will pass a hill on the right, once topped with an ancient fort. Continue to reach a padlocked gate on the left. You can make a diversion here. Climb the gate and walk up the track, passing two ponds to reach a house.

⑤ Turn right on the grassy track and walk back on yourself, going through a gate in a deer fence, then past several pheasant feeders. Go through another gate at the bottom, turn left and return to the road.

⑥ If you've done the diversion, turn left, if not, continue following the road, which now starts to wind

downhill. You'll soon reach an electricity sub station and mobile phone mast, from where you'll get good views of Finavon Castle. When you reach some houses, turn right.

WHERE TO EAT AND DRINK ⓘ

There are several places to choose from in nearby Forfar. The **Royal Hotel** serves lunches such as sandwiches, filled baguettes and baked potatoes, as well as dishes like lasagne and vegetable curry. It also offers substantial evening meals such as steak-and-Guinness pie and haggis.

---

⑦ Walk past **Bogardo house** and follow the track as it swings left between fields. Turn right at the gap and cross the field, then go right again at the next field edge. At the top of the field go left and walk to the far end. You'll now have to scramble over a watery, overgrown ditch and climb over a barbed-wire fence.

⑧ Maintain direction, walking on the pasture to the right of the fence (the track is overgrown). At the end, turn left through a gate and continue along the obvious track, to pass **Woodrae**. Continue to pass an old dovecote on the left, then turn right at the road. Walk uphill, past **Balbinny** and to the junction. Turn right to return to **Aberlemno**.

WHILE YOU'RE THERE ⓘ

Glamis Castle is a few miles away and well worth a visit. The seat of the Earls of Strathmore and childhood home of the late Queen Elizabeth, the Queen Mother, it is a wonderfully atmospheric castle, with towers, turrets and tiny windows. It is also said to be haunted by a 'grey lady' who appears in the chapel. You can take a tour of the castle and also visit the grounds and café.

An Extension to Turin Hill

A longer walk from Aberlemno to an ancient fort.
See map and information panel for Walk 48

•DISTANCE•	5 miles (8km)
•MINIMUM TIME•	2hrs 45min
•ASCENT / GRADIENT•	768ft (234m) ▲▲▲
•LEVEL OF DIFFICULTY•	🚶🚶 🚶🚶 🚶

Walk 49 Directions (Walk 48 option)

At the road corner, after passing the entrance to **Woodside**, take the stony track that bears left. Follow it in front of some farm buildings. When you reach a road, turn left and follow the track past **Turin Hill Farm** (Point Ⓐ). Go through the rusty gate and keep ahead across the field. Go through another gate and pass a patch of woodland on the right. You soon reach a gate on the left saying 'Bull in field' (Point Ⓑ). Climb this (with care, it's electrified) then walk ahead across the pasture (sheep were in it when I was here) to go round the margin of the wood ahead.

Go through another gate (there's an electric fence in front of it) and continue walking uphill to reach a wall on the very top of the **Turin Hill** (Point Ⓒ). There are great views here over the surrounding countryside. You can turn left now to see the remains of **Kemp's Castle**, an ancient fort.

Retrace your steps, back past the wood and across the pasture and over the gates. Walk down to pass the farmhouse again, then keep on the metalled track. Ignore the turning on the right-hand side (Point Ⓓ) and walk ahead to join the main road – the **B9134**. Turn right and continue until you see a turning on the left signed 'Finavon Hill'. You now rejoin the main walk at Point ③.

WHILE YOU'RE THERE

Arbroath is a short drive from Aberlemno and worth visiting for its famous abbey. This was founded in 1178 by William the Lion and it became an extremely wealthy monastery. It was in the abbey in 1320 that Scottish nobles signed the Declaration of Arbroath, in which Scotland's noblemen affirmed allegiance to Robert the Bruce. The document asked the Pope to reverse its excommunication of Bruce and recognise him as King of Scotland. The document is a clear assertion of Scotland's nationhood and independence from England and contains the famous lines:

'...for as long as but a hundred of us remain alive, never will we on any conditions be brought under English rule. It is in truth not for glory, nor riches, nor honours that we fight, but for freedom – for that alone, which no honest man gives up but with life itself...'

The Pope eventually agreed to their wishes. The words in the Declaration of Arbroath later provided the basis for America's Declaration of Independence.

Walk 50

Dunnottar's Hidden Treasure

A lovely walk along the cliffs to Dunnottar Castle.

•DISTANCE•	3½ miles (5.7km)
•MINIMUM TIME•	1hr 30min
•ASCENT / GRADIENT•	377ft (115m) ▲▲▲
•LEVEL OF DIFFICULTY•	林 林 林
•PATHS•	Cliff edges, metalled tracks and forest paths, 3 stiles
•LANDSCAPE•	Striking seascapes and ancient castle
•SUGGESTED MAP•	aqua3 OS Pathfinder 273 Stonehaven, Inverbervie & Lawrencekirk
•START / FINISH•	Grid reference: NO 874858
•DOG FRIENDLINESS•	On lead along cliffs
•PARKING•	Market Square in Stonehaven
•PUBLIC TOILETS•	By Market Square

Walk 50 Directions

Scotland's Crown Jewels are among the oldest in Europe. Also known as the Honours of Scotland, they comprise a crown, made in 1540 of gold encrusted with precious stones and pearls, a sword of state, and a silver sceptre. Today they are on display at Edinburgh Castle, but you can only see them thanks to the bravery of the people who hid them from Cromwell's army.

From the **Market Square** in Stonehaven, walk back on to **Allardyce Street**, turn right and cross over the road. Turn left along **Market Lane** and, at the beach, turn

WHERE TO EAT AND DRINK ⓘ

The **Ship Inn** by the harbour serves food all day from noon at the weekends. The **Marine Hotel** near by serves lunches from noon to 2PM and supper from 5–9:15PM. You can also try the **Carron Restaurant** which has seats outside and serves seafood, baguettes, baked potatoes and toasties.

right to cross the footbridge. Your route now takes you along duckboards beside the beach, then past a wire sculpture of a dolphin. Turn right at the signs to Dunnottar Castle, which bring you out at the little harbour.

During the 18th century the harbour was the focus of trade in Stonehaven. Grain, potatoes, whisky and fish were the main exports, while coal and lime were the main imports. Cross here to continue down **Shorehead**. Pass the **Marine Hotel**, then turn right into **Wallis Wynd** and left into **Castle Street**. It's a bit of a puff uphill now, but you're soon rewarded with great views over the harbour. You emerge at the main road, then maintain direction, walking along the road until it bends. Continue ahead, following the enclosed tarmac track. This takes you between arable fields and past a **war memorial** on the right-hand side. Your path soon gets narrower and you will see signs saying that erosion has made it hazardous (though it is still widely used). You pass another bay on the left-hand side and will get great views of both the castle ahead and of the seabirds swooping over the cliffs. Nip over the stile at the end of the track and make your way across the middle of a field, then cross a footbridge and two more stiles. You now pass a track going down to **Castle Haven Bay** and continue, following the main path around the cliff edge. Cross another footbridge and bear uphill. The path is laced with wild flowers and the seaweed down in the bay creates a rich, salty collage of copper, ochre and green. You'll soon reach some steps on your left that run down to **Dunnottar Castle**.

The Scottish regalia had been taken to the castle when Cromwell invaded Scotland. He intended to destroy them as he had done with the English Crown Jewels, and they were spirited away from Edinburgh for safe keeping. Cromwell came to Dunnottar and beseiged the castle for nearly a year, but when it finally fell the jewels had gone. They had been smuggled out by the wife of the local minister and her maid, who had hidden the jewels in their clothes. The Honours were then hidden for eight years in the church at nearby Kinneff, and returned to Edinburgh after the Restoration. This wasn't the end of their travails however. Now nominally safe in

Scotland's capital, the Honours were hidden away after the Act of Union, and walled up in a sealed room. People eventually forgot where they were and many believed they had been stolen by the English. Sir Walter Scott rediscovered them, locked inside a dusty chest.

Your walk bears right here, past a waterfall, through a kissing gate and up to a house. Pass the house to reach the main road, turn right, then take the first turning on the left, walking in the direction of the radio masts. Follow this wide, metalled track past the masts and on past **East Newtonleys** on the left-hand side. When you reach the main **A957**, turn right and walk downhill, then take the first turning on the left-hand side. Follow this track to reach a sign on the right saying 'Carron Gate'. Turn right and walk through the woods, following the lower path on the right-hand side that runs by the burn.

You'll soon reach a little **Shell House** on the left, built in the 19th century for the children of the local gentry. It gets its name – not surprisingly – from the thousands of seashells that decorate its interior. Passing this on the left, continue along the lower track, then climb uphill to join a wider track. Bear right here, to maintain direction and reach the edge of the woods. Walk through the housing estate to join **Low Wood Road** and the river. Turn left, then right to cross the footbridge with the green railings. Turn right and walk by the water. You'll soon pass the striking Art Deco **Carron Restaurant** on the left-hand side, and will reach a cream-coloured iron bridge. Bear left here, then turn first right to return to the **Market Square**.

> **WHILE YOU'RE THERE** ⓘ
> Further down the coast is **Kineff Old Church**, where the Scottish Crown Jewels were hidden under the church floor in 1651. There's a memorial at the church to the Revd James Granger who, with his wife, was responsible for hiding the treasures and thus saving them for Scotland. Sometimes they kept them under their bed instead of in the church.

Walking in Safety

All these walks are suitable for any reasonably fit person, but less experienced walkers should try the easier walks first. Route finding is usually straightforward, but you will find that an Ordnance Survey map is a useful addition to the route maps and descriptions.

Risks

Although each walk here has been researched with a view to minimising the risks to the walkers who follow its route, no walk in the countryside can be considered to be completely free from risk. Walking in the outdoors will always require a degree of common sense and judgement to ensure that it is as safe as possible.

- Be particularly careful on cliff paths and in upland terrain, where the consequences of a slip can be very serious.

- Remember to check tidal conditions before walking on the seashore.

- Some sections of route are by, or cross, busy roads. Take care and remember traffic is a danger even on minor country lanes.

- Be careful around farmyard machinery and livestock, especially if you have children with you.

- Be aware of the consequences of changes in the weather and check the forecast before you set out. Carry spare clothing and a torch if you are walking in the winter months. Remember the weather can change very quickly at any time of the year, and in moorland and heathland areas, mist and fog can make route finding much harder. Don't set out in these conditions unless you are confident of your navigation skills in poor visibility. In summer remember to take account of the heat and sun; wear a hat and carry spare water.

- On walks away from centres of population you should carry a whistle and survival bag. If you do have an accident requiring the emergency services, make a note of your position as accurately as possible and dial 999.

Acknowledgements

The author would like to thank the following people for joining her on the hills in the rain – Fiona Ballantyne, Elizabeth Cunningham, Cavan Convery, Annemarie Gibson, Shelagh Green, Edward Longbottom, Gill MacAskill and, above all, Billy O'Reilly. Thanks also to Mum and Dad for their unfailing support.

AQUA3 AA Publishing and Outcrop Publishing Services would like to thank Chartech for supplying aqua3 maps for this book.
For more information visit their website: www.aqua3.com.

Series management: Outcrop Publishing Services Limited, Cumbria
Series editor: Chris Bagshaw **Copy editor:** Jenni Davis
Front cover: www.BritainonView.com **Back cover:** AA Photo Library/J Martin